creating your perfect

WEDDING

creating your perfect
WEDDING

stylish ideas and step-by-step projects for a beautiful wedding

Lucinda Ganderton
with projects by **Sania Pell**

RYLAND
PETERS
& SMALL
LONDON NEW YORK

DESIGNER Sonya Nathoo
SENIOR EDITOR Annabel Morgan
PICTURE AND LOCATION RESEARCH
Emily Westlake
PRODUCTION Gemma Moules
ART DIRECTOR Gabriella Le Grazie
PUBLISHING DIRECTOR Alison Starling

First published in the UK in 2005 by
Ryland Peters & Small
20–21 Jockey's Fields
London WC1R 4BW
www.rylandpeters.com

10 9 8 7 6 5 4 3 2 1

ISBN 1 84172 939 6

Printed and bound in China.

contents

Introduction

Every wedding is unique – a celebration of the romance between the bride and groom, and a joyful occasion when friends and family come together to share their mutual happiness. Whether you are planning a traditional, formal event with a grand reception, or a simple service with only a handful of people in attendance, your wedding should be enjoyable, memorable and just as individual as you are.

Creating a perfect, magical wedding is not reliant on unlimited funds or extravagant flourishes. Amidst all the ceremony, it will be the attention to detail that stands out and that will linger in the memory of your guests. Exercising your creativity on these fine details should be an enjoyable process and it's a compliment to everyone who attends your wedding to make the day as beautiful as it can be. There's no set formula for success. You can tailor your wedding to suit your taste and budget, even if much of the organization is being delegated to a wedding planner.

This book brings together a wealth of creative ideas, all of which will inspire you to add a personal touch to your festivities and to make your wedding day entirely your own. Along with the enchanting and easy-to-achieve step-by-step projects, there are pages of gorgeous flowers, suggestions for table settings, ideas for thoughtful favours and romantic keepsakes, and special souvenirs for you and your guests to treasure.

Wedding flowers

Flowers are a vital ingredient at any wedding – their colourful petals bring fragrance, drama and a sense of romance to the celebration. There are so many beautiful blooms to choose from – delicate silky-petalled sweet peas, regal lilies, luscious full-blown roses or dainty lily of the valley are just a few of the favourites. Whichever you pick, be sure to carry the theme from the bride's bouquet and the groom's buttonhole through to the table arrangements and chair backs at the reception.

ABOVE A domed bouquet
needs little extra adornment:
here, a luscious bow of bronze
satin provides the perfect foil
for a densely packed bunch
of yellow Illios roses.

RIGHT Pristine white roses
are complemented by swirling
loops of wire-edged gauzy
ribbon in a metallic bronze.

bridal bouquets

Whether the wedding theme is traditional, minimalist, formal or casual, every
bride is certain to carry a bouquet on her wedding day. Dreamy, sensuous and
fragrant, the bridal flowers should be an expression of their bearer's personality
as well as the perfect complement to her gown. As with wedding dresses,
fashions in bouquets have changed over the years. Looking back through any
family album will reveal structured, formal bouquets that can look stiff to
modern eyes. Contemporary bouquets tend to be more informal. They are
usually hand-tied and use a wider choice of flowers than ever before.

FAR LEFT Imported roses are now available all year round. For this autumnal bouquet they are combined with berries, oak leaves and kumquats.

LEFT Delicate, fragrant lily of the valley is the most charming of all spring flowers. When grouped en masse, as here, the effect (and scent) is stunning. The flowers are encircled by their own glossy green leaves.

ABOVE The availability of tulips is also no longer restricted to a short flowering season: nowadays, their rich colours and perfect petals can brighten the cooler months too.

ABOVE The very best fabric flowers are hard to distinguish from fresh blooms: the veining and shading on the petals and leaves of these pink roses is subtly authentic. A silk bouquet can be treasured for many years.

ABOVE RIGHT An old-fashioned favourite, anemones are now enjoying a revival. The shell-pink petals of this unusual variety contrast graphically with the charcoal centres, a colour that is echoed in the lavish organza ribbon.

RIGHT All-white wedding flowers are a traditional choice, but this informal garden bouquet is unmistakably contemporary. The stems are bound with ribbon and secured with pearl-headed pins (as shown on pages 16–17).

FAR RIGHT This romantic round arrangement is assembled from a skilfully chosen mixture of flowers, which all fall within the same narrow colour range. It is another example of the trend towards minimum foliage within a bouquet.

TOP The flowers in this sophisticated, structured bouquet were chosen for both their fragrance and their colour: ranunculus, delicate sweet peas, and deep-red roses. Any extra foliage would have detracted from the effect.

ABOVE Here is a truly sentimental Victorian-style posy: according to *The Language of Flowers*, forget-me-nots embody 'true love' and pansies 'tender and pleasant thoughts'.

RIGHT Yellow and purple oppose each other on the colour spectrum, giving any arrangement that includes them an added vibrancy. This pairing of sunflowers and cornflowers is the perfect choice for a summer wedding.

FAR RIGHT Like other exotic blooms, these Singapore orchids have intensely coloured, intricately shaped petals. Bunched together with a binding of ruffled satin ribbon, they make a tactile, eye-catching bouquet.

BELOW These purple and cream lilac branches will fill the air with their heady perfume. They are informally tied at the top with a wide satin ribbon, leaving the dark, woody stems uncovered.

A wedding bouquet is the one accessory no bride can be without.

Although wiring is still used to give some support, the structure now comes from the flowers and foliage themselves. As a rule, the more tailored the outfit, the more structured the bouquet should be: a slinky sheath demands nothing more than a few exquisite blooms, while a full skirt is better balanced with the lush informality of a lavish bouquet.

Most species are now available all year round, but seasonal flowers have their own particular charm and, more prosaically, are less costly. Spring is a time for delicate, fragrant flowers, while summer offers a wealth of choice in myriad colours and shapes. Autumn and winter foliage is striking: copper beech, holly, berries and ivy (whose tendrils represent 'wedded love') will all complement a wide range of flowers.

THIS PICTURE Unlike its fragile cousins, the Iceland poppy is a robust cut flower that makes an exuberant, colourful and unusual bouquet.

FAR LEFT A moss-filled rustic willow basket will keep its contents fresh throughout the long day and can be carried easily.

LEFT An appealing combination of lilies of the valley and sweet violets is given a new twist with trailing ribbons and sequins.

hand-tied bouquets

An arrangement of a single bloom has great impact, and these bouquets show the flowers off to their best advantage. Choose flowers with perfect petals and, if necessary, give the cut stems a quick blast with a hairdryer to prevent any sap leaking. The stalks of the bridal bouquet are bound and pinned with ribbon, while the bridesmaid's flowers have been more informally tied with lace and velvet to complement her dress.

MATERIALS & EQUIPMENT

BRIDE'S BOUQUET
1m of 6cm-wide satin ribbon
Pearl-headed pins • Floristry wire
Scissors • Secateurs

BRIDESMAID'S BOUQUET
30cm of 6cm-wide satin ribbon
30cm lace trim
50cm of 1cm-wide velvet ribbon
Pearl-headed pin • Matching bead
Scissors • Secateurs

1 Ensure the stems are clean, then carefully remove any thorns or surplus leaves (wearing gloves if necessary). Arrange the flowers together in a domed bunch, holding them close to their heads, and bind the stems with wire.

2 Cut 20cm of ribbon and fold under one end. Wrap it around the stems and pin in place, slanting the pin downwards. Repeat four more times, overlapping each ribbon, and trim the stems in line with the bottom edge.

1 Hold the flowers in a bunch, just below their heads, and shape them into a rounded dome. Keeping them in this position, secure the stems with floristry wire or a piece of lace and trim the stems to the same length.

2 Place the strip of lace on the satin ribbon and wrap them around the stems. Pin the edges together at the back. Tie the velvet ribbon into a bow at the front. Thread the bead on to the pin and push it through the knot to finish.

attendants' flowers

The flowers that the bridal attendants carry or wear should continue the overall theme of the wedding and harmonize with the bride's bouquet. The arrangements do not all have to be exactly the same, however – several different groupings of the same flowers will look more interesting than identical bouquets. When choosing the size and shape of their individual arrangements, bear in mind the age of the bridesmaids and flower girls. Grown-up attendants may be happy to hold a bouquet throughout the day, but little fingers tend to get fidgety. Consider tightly bound posies, baskets, floral hoops or pompom-like flower balls as an option for the youngest bridesmaids.

TOP LEFT Bridesmaids' flowers need not always be on a smaller scale than the bride's bouquet. These pretty complementary hand-tied bouquets for a bride and her attendant are distinguished by using different types of foliage for each one. The bridesmaid also has sprigs of jasmine pinned in her loosely flowing hair.

TOP CENTRE A stylish and fashionable corsage for an attendant is created by stitching a single hydrangea head to a length of woven braid.

TOP RIGHT Blue and purple spring flowers – forget-me-nots and pansies – in a simple posy for an older attendant. Their intense colour is emphasized by loops of shiny satin ribbon.

CENTRE Daisies, with their attributes of beauty and innocence, have long been a favourite choice for younger attendants. The pink and white varieties used here have been combined with forget-me-nots to colourful effect.

BOTTOM LEFT Two delightful posies in spring shades of lime, apple and yellow green, framed with dark ivy. One is arranged in precise concentric rings, like a 'tussie-mussie', while the other is a more haphazard grouping.

BOTTOM RIGHT Tiny bridesmaids should be given flowers that are easy to carry and relatively robust. These pompom-shaped hydrangea balls and matching circlets should withstand a modicum of wear and tear.

buttonholes

Just as most brides carry a bouquet, the majority of grooms sport a buttonhole in the lapel of their wedding suits. This flower arrangement in miniature usually takes its cue from the flowers that make up the bridal bouquet. The stems of the chosen flowers are trimmed then bound with florist's tape, which can be camouflaged with pretty ribbon or braid. A single rose is the classic choice for a buttonhole, but there are a wealth of other decorative possibilities that will look equally elegant.

ABOVE LEFT This combination of yellow and white freesia and irises set off by a spray of mimosa would bring a breath of fresh air to a spring wedding.

ABOVE CENTRE A demure little cluster of grape hyacinths is reminiscent of a Victorian posy. The flowers are encircled with glossy galax leaves and bound with a criss-crossed blue ribbon.

ABOVE RIGHT The bright yellow centres of the tiny chamomile flowers pick up the colour of the tightly furled petals of the ranunculus heads.

RIGHT The stem of this flawless pink-edged Candy Bianca rosebud has been bound with tape to conceal the wired ivy leaf supports, then embellished with a twirl of fine flowery braid.

The groom's buttonhole may be a floral arrangement in miniature or a compact single bloom, but the flowers should always echo those in the bridal bouquet.

ABOVE LEFT If the bride is carrying an exotic bouquet, the groom's buttonhole can subtly pick up on the same theme. Discreetly spectacular, this velvet-textured burnt-orange cockscomb makes a ruffled collar for a rich apricot rosebud.

ABOVE RIGHT Here, the groom's buttonhole (below) is fashioned from a luscious deep red Grand Prix rose and a spray of winter jasmine trimmed with a toning satin bow. The other male members of the bridal party have buttonholes that are a variation on the same colour scheme, concocted from Martinique roses turned inside out and wrapped in galax leaves.

LEFT A single, perfect white rose is the traditional buttonhole. This one, with its petals just starting to unfurl, looks classically elegant against the dark suiting of the groom's lapel.

PROJECT 2
floral headpiece

This elegant confection is a stylish reworking of the traditional flowered headband and net veil combination. The headpiece would look perfect with either a formal or informal wedding outfit, and will complement any hairstyle – upswept or down, long or short. The delicate flowers are cut from paper-like silk taffeta (you could make them from remnants from the bride's dress), then trimmed with glittering diamantés and threaded on crystal bead stamens and attached to a comb. The flirtatious net trimming and slender feather quills add a final flourish.

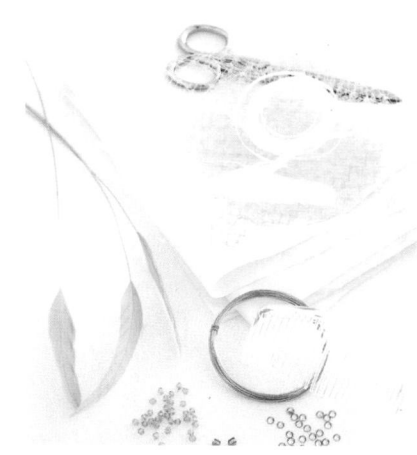

MATERIALS & EQUIPMENT
Tracing paper and pencil • Length of cream silk taffeta
or similar non-fraying fabric, approximately 40 x 50cm
Scissors • 16 x 4mm stick-on diamantés • Clear adhesive
Floristry wire • Wire cutters • 60 x 8mm glass beads
3 x 30cm lilac feather quills
4 x 20cm white feather quills
10cm-wide clear plastic hair comb • 1m of 4mm-wide ribbon
Needle and sewing thread
20 x 30cm rectangle of net with curved corners

1   Cut one large, six medium and six small petals from your silk, using the templates on page 111. Fold each in half then into quarters and eighths, pressing along the creases. Snip the tip to make a hole. Glue one diamanté to each petal.

2 Thread three glass beads on to a 20cm length of wire. Pass the end back through the last two beads and twist it firmly beneath the beads. Make nineteen more stamens in the same way, then twist them together in four groups of five.

3 Assemble the petals into four flowers. Thread a stamen through the centre of each. Hold the feathers along the back of the comb and bind the wires around the comb to attach the flowers, starting with the smallest.

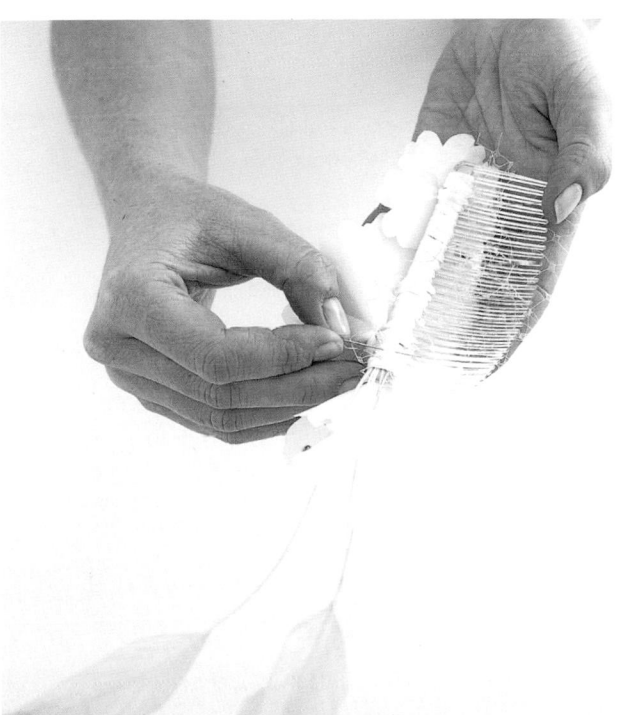

4 Starting at the outside edge, wrap the ribbon neatly over and under the top of the comb, passing it below the flowers and in between the teeth to conceal the wire and quills. Trim any loose ends and stitch them down.

5 Position the net veil at the front of the comb, beneath the edge of the flowers. Sew the two corners down, then hand-stitch the net to the ribbon, working from the wrong side. Pleat the net as necessary to fit it all on to the comb.

table flowers

The floral theme of a wedding is generally set by the bride's flowers. The flowers and colours of her bouquet will set the style for other flowers displayed at the reception. Whether the wedding is a formal sit-down meal, a relaxed buffet or a country-style garden party, fresh flowers will add to the enjoyment of your guests and enhance the table settings.

Once you have decided on a general theme and colour scheme for the wedding, your choice of flowers will follow on naturally. Before you start to plan the flowers in any detail, it's sensible to visit the location and take note of the size and proportions of the space, the number of tables and the way in which you would like them to be set out on the day.

RIGHT Tiny sprays of silvery green foliage break up the solid mass of these closely packed rosebuds.

BELOW RIGHT Choosing the correct container is as important as selecting the right flowers. This pewter dish is ideal for a short-stemmed, domed group of pink roses and stephanotis.

BOTTOM RIGHT This shallow dish of cream roses and green lady's mantle makes a pretty, informal centrepiece, ideal for a summer wedding.

Floral centrepieces are the main focus of the tables your guests will dine at, but they should not be so large in scale or so dramatic that they block the view across the table or prevent guests from socializing. Tall, structured arrangements are very striking, and can transform even the humblest of settings, but they are best saved for a position where everyone can appreciate them – in alcoves or set on pedestals. Attractive architectural features, such as deep windowsills or ornate mantelpieces, are also ideal spots to position larger-scale displays.

BELOW This beautiful outdoor setting, surrounded by lawn and trees, requires little more embellishment than a few perfect hydrangea heads artlessly grouped in a plain glass vase, and a border of trailing ivy and eucharis lilies pinned to the edge of the table.

ABOVE RIGHT Single roses stand to attention in a row of bud vases. One will be positioned at each setting.

RIGHT The elegant, sculptural lines of these calla lilies are exploited by being arranged simply in a clear glass vase.

OPPOSITE, MAIN PICTURE A luscious sugar-pink peony and a full-blown rose in the same shade float ethereally within a glass globe. Goldfish bowls make spectacular centrepieces, and are also economical, requiring just a couple of perfect specimens to create a huge impact.

OPPOSITE, INSET A single rosebud sits in a tall, slender wineglass. This witty individual arrangement is repeated at every place setting.

LEFT An outside setting always demands informality: this spontaneous grouping of flowers and berries seems to spill out of its bucket container as it glows in the intense sunlight of a late-summer garden wedding.

BELOW Paper White narcissi and hyacinth heads create a delicate effect when arranged in whitewashed terracotta flowerpots. They bring an air of simplicity to the starched linen and silver-topped cruets of a formal table.

Your table flowers should take their cue from the size, shape and number of tables. Round tables are ideally suited to one dramatic central arrangement, while rectangular tables can look very effective decorated with a dainty individual posy at each setting, which can double up as a favour or place-card holder. Take advantage of a single long trestle table by decorating it with a long line of vases of alternating sizes running down the centre of the table. Good natural lighting is a bonus for a daytime reception, and an evening meal will benefit from carefully thought-out candlelight, which could be incorporated into the flower arrangements.

LEFT Nowadays, artificial flowers look just as good as the real thing, but they are much easier to care for and last a lot longer! Here, a single perfect silk bloom and a tightly furled bud welcome the guests to their places at the dining table.

BELOW An already romantic setting for an outdoor reception is given a fairy-tale quality by garlanding the rustic columns with ivy and roses. The red and green colour scheme continues with the suitably low-level floral centrepiece.

Round tables are ideally suited to one dramatic central arrangement.

RIGHT An old wooden garden bench is dressed up with a generous cluster of pastel-coloured roses, crab apples, feverfew and other garden flowers.

CENTRE RIGHT This garland has been created by bending flexible branches of golden mimosa into a circle and binding them together at intervals with florist's wire.

BELOW LEFT Ribbed green hosta leaves tenderly enfold old-fashioned pinks and summer roses. The posy is tied with satin ribbon and wired to a folding garden chair.

BELOW RIGHT This glorious chair-back wreath was made by wiring lengths of ivy and anemone heads on to a ready-made twig wreath, available from good florists. Match the ribbon to the colour of the petals.

chair backs

Floral chair-back decorations are a charming finishing touch to a wedding reception, whether it is held indoors or outside. Small garlands, large hoops or compact sprays can be used to adorn the back of every seat, or just those at the high table. Scented flowers will perfume the air throughout the meal, and add to the enjoyment of your guests. Make sure, however, that each arrangement is attached securely and positioned so that it will not become damaged when the occupant of the chair is seated.

ABOVE RIGHT This white card cornucopia (an ancient symbol of fertility) has been filled with evergreen foliage and feathery flower heads, and suspended by a cream ribbon.

RIGHT Elegant spindle-backed gilt chairs like these are easily obtained from hire companies. Make the bride and groom's seats stand out even more by adorning them with tumbling cascades of flowers.

PROJECT 3
wreath of flowers

This exuberant wreath is fashioned from greenish-pink hydrangeas and studded with sugar-pink roses. It is not too large or cumbersome, so could be carried by a flower girl as an alternative to a posy, or used to decorate a door or windowframe. The wreath should ideally be made on the day so that the flowers retain their freshness, but if it has to be put together in advance, be sure to soak the oasis ring in water for an hour first. At the end of the evening, the wreath can be put away in a cool place to allow it to dry out and become a long-lasting keepsake.

MATERIALS & EQUIPMENT
Oasis ring, 30cm in diameter
150cm length of medium-width gauzy ribbon
Secateurs or heavy-duty scissors
10 hydrangea heads • 15 roses
About 30 large sequins, 15mm in diameter
Floristry wire • Wire cutters
15 silk or feather butterflies

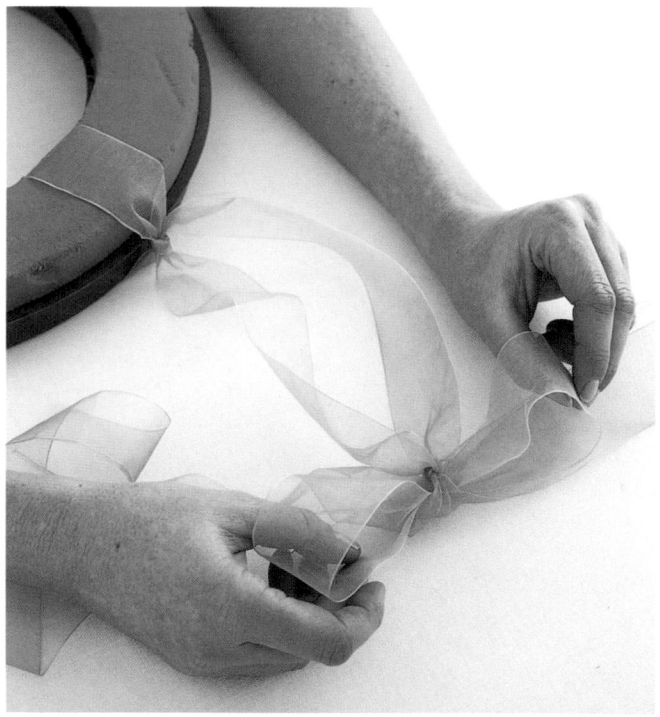

1   Slip the ribbon through the oasis ring and knot in place, making sure that the two ends are the same length. Tie them into a bow, 20cm from the ring, adjusting the loops so that they are equal, then trim the ends of the ribbon neatly.

2   Cut the hydrangeas into individual sprays, discarding any flowers that are damaged or discoloured. Push the stalks firmly into the oasis, all around the ring, so that the flowers conceal the top and side edges of the ring completely.

3   Trim the rose stems down to about 12cm and add them to the wreath, pushing them in between the hydrangeas. Arrange them in five evenly spaced groups of three, to give maximum impact.

4   Position a sequin 4cm from the end of a 15cm length of wire. Bend over the short end and twist around the long end. Do the same with the other sequins and add wires to the butterflies if they are not already wired.

5   Insert the wired butterflies at intervals around the edge of the garland, so they appear to be perching there. Push the sequin wires amongst the hydrangeas and roses in small clusters, so they catch the light as they move.

Wedding cakes

The traditional wedding cake, balanced on plaster pillars
and topped with tiny figurines of the bride and groom,
has in recent years been reworked into a delectable new
confection of layered tiers, fresh flowers, ribbons and
different flavours. But one thing will never change –
the cake will always have pride of place at the wedding
reception, where it is first displayed for the admiration
of the guests, then later cut and shared among them.

The bride and groom cut the wedding cake together to symbolize their shared future.

LEFT AND CENTRE LEFT Fresh flowers that tie in with the bride's bouquet can be used to add colour instead of bright icing. Here, a posy of pink and red roses and purple lavender sits on each tier of this cake, with a full-blown bloom perched at the very top.

BOTTOM LEFT In a radical departure from tradition, this cone-shaped cake is swathed with ruffled ribbons of glossy chocolate. Pastel flowers would be overwhelmed by such richness, so the cake is adorned with vivid pink, red and blue anemones to create a bold effect.

A magnificent multi-tiered cake provides an important focal point at the wedding reception, and the ceremonial cutting of the cake is more than just another photo opportunity; like so many other wedding rituals, the wedding cake has a long history. It is traditionally baked from a rich mixture including exotic spices, nuts and dried 'fruits of the earth' to represent fertility. Each layer is covered with marzipan and finished off with a thick coating of white icing – white being the colour of purity. The top tier is often set aside to await the birth of a child or to celebrate the first anniversary of the wedding. Many brides still continue the custom of sending a small box of cake to those who were unable to

FAR LEFT White-on-white icing is elegant and understated. This brocade effect is created by piping small swirls and dots on to a smooth iced background, and the texture is emphasized by the bands of pearl-covered braid.

ABOVE Perfect pink hydrangeas and stephanotis decorate this layered cake. A dome of flowers caps the top tier, and posies cascade down one side. The icing pearls at the base of each tier contribute to the exquisite effect.

THIS PAGE One simple stacked cake is shown two ways. Studded with artificial flowers and a trailing organza bow, the cake has a softer look; it appears more formal when decorated with bands of wide satin ribbon (inset above).

BELOW LEFT This ultra-feminine confection in cool shades of shell pink is iced with an interwoven pattern and finished off with fresh roses, so that it resembles a stack of flower-filled baskets. The three square cakes can easily be cut into neat, evenly sized slices.

BELOW RIGHT Skilfully modelled sugar flowers, such as these naturalistic rosebuds complete with leaves, are almost indistinguishable from the real thing. They add a look of classic sophistication to a plain white-iced cake. A surprisingly wide range of moulds and cutters to stamp out different-shaped leaves and petals can be found in specialist cake-making shops, along with ready-made icing for modelling, colourings and stamens.

attend the celebrations. Such a gift can be particularly welcome: superstition has it that an unmarried girl who sleeps with the crumbs under her pillow will dream of her future husband.

Contemporary wedding cakes are varied and exciting. Not everybody likes fruit cake, and you may need to consider special dietary requirements, so cakes in which each tier is different are increasingly popular: pick and mix from lemon sponge, chocolate gateau, carrot cake or a fat-free sponge, all of which can be decorated as you wish. Alternatively you could opt for a French croquembouche (a pile of choux pastry buns), a pyramid of meringues, or – a key trend – individual cupcakes with bright icing or sugar flowers arranged on a tiered cake stand.

ABOVE LEFT, CENTRE AND RIGHT Each of the tiers that make up this gorgeous cake has been edged with rolled white chocolate as a delicious substitute for the more usual icing. The cake is topped with a ruffled chocolate rosette. The delicate butterfly ornaments that hover above each layer are the perfect finishing touches.

LEFT Tempting mouthfuls for the sweet of tooth: tiny fondant cakes in fluted paper cases can be piped with stripes, flowers or a monogram. You may, however, need to allow more than one per guest, as they will undoubtedly prove irresistible.

RIGHT Individual fairy cakes are an increasingly popular alternative to the conventional wedding cake. They can be iced with colours and motifs to fit in with any theme – these enticing versions are embellished with pastel hearts and flowers – then set out on a cake stand or large plate.

Superstition has it that an unmarried girl who sleeps with crumbs of wedding cake under her pillow will dream of her future husband.

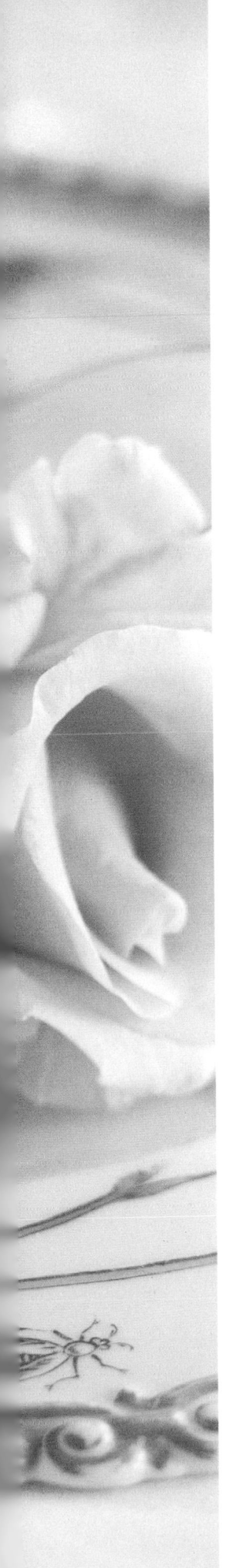

Table settings

After the formality of the wedding ceremony, the reception is a time for festivity and entertainment. Family and friends have come to join together in celebration of your marriage, so create a welcoming atmosphere that lets your guests know how much you appreciate their presence. The wedding meal should be a visual delight, so plan beautifully decorated tables adorned with details that they will enjoy throughout the celebration.

Classic white napkins are the ultimate table accessory, and can be dressed up or down to match the theme of any wedding.

THIS PAGE Mother-of-pearl buttons and tiny pearl beads, all in pure white, have been selected to complement the textured stitching on these embroidered cotton napkins.

napkins

White napery – the archaic term for tablecloths and napkins – is a traditional choice for weddings. Crisply starched linen or self-patterned damask provides the perfect backdrop for cutlery, crockery, flowers and glassware, preventing the table from appearing cluttered. For effect, coloured napkins, especially those in pastel shades, are a good way of picking up the wedding colour scheme. The way in which the napkins are presented – rolled, folded or tied – adds the final decorative flourish.

RIGHT These striking napkin rings, constructed from coiled gilt wire, have been chosen to match a dining service with a gold-coloured glaze.

ABOVE LEFT Tiny sprays of lavender, tied up with raffia and tucked under bands of narrow organza ribbon, will release their scent as the napkins are unfolded.

ABOVE CENTRE Hand-lettered name tags, made from simple rectangles of card, are tied on to silver filigree rings with short lengths of white velvet ribbon.

ABOVE RIGHT These loosely rolled napkins are bound with simple ties of gauzy ribbon. Use wire edged organza, which retains its shape when twisted into knots.

Most caterers will supply table linen as part of their package, but if you are having a wedding at home, or would like to provide your own linen, search for vintage napkins in flea markets and local auctions. Look out for pretty, unusual details, such as delicate lace edgings, embroidery, monograms and hemstitching. Linen and cotton napkins can be restored to pristine whiteness by boil-washing and starching: old linen always improves with laundering, which enhances the texture of the fine fabric.

TOP Three ways with a hemstitched napkin: folded in half then pleated and tied with velvet ribbon; with opposite corners rolled towards the centre and secured with a rose hair-tie; folded into thirds with a place card slipped under the top layer.

ABOVE LEFT A napkin folded into quarters and tied at the corner with velvet ribbon holds a spray of autumn berries.

LEFT Porcelain napkin rings are paired with fine damask at the bride and groom's settings.

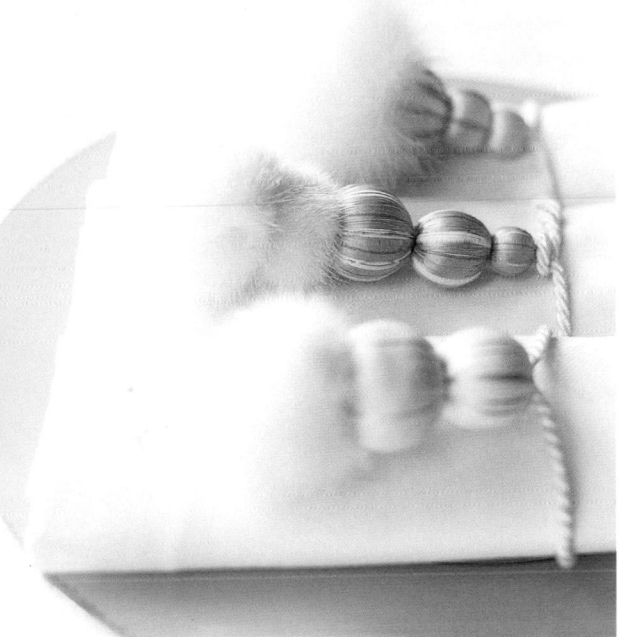

ABOVE LEFT Choose plain napkins and accessorize them with individual ties to set off beautiful china: this silver bead and diamanté tassel is the perfect foil for a delicate silver-edged plate.

ABOVE RIGHT Scour haberdashers and furnishing departments for trims and tassels that can double up as quirky napkin ties. The fur trim on these elegant examples would add glamour to a winter wedding.

LEFT Another tiny dessert napkin – this time a fine linen square with a prettily scalloped edge – is cinched with a neat circle of embroidered petersham ribbon. Use woven upholstery braid for a similar effect.

FAR LEFT After the main meal comes the ceremonial cutting of the cake. Provide guests with a pastry fork and a fresh napkin, held together with a band of pink ribbon.

RIGHT Reminiscent of a more elegant era,
a floral china cup and saucer complete with
dainty lace-edged napkin set the scene for
coffee and petits fours.

ABOVE A junk-shop find, this linen napkin
is decorated with spring flowers. Search for
similar napkins to set out on cake or dessert
plates. They don't all have to be the same –
quirky mismatching napkins look very cute.

Rules of etiquette dictate that the more formal the occasion,
the larger the napkins should be. Some antique examples are up
to a metre square in size. Often these were folded into intricate
shapes – fans, lilies or, especially for weddings, lovers' knots.
Once the guests were seated, the napkins were unfolded and
refolded across the lap, so a double layer of fabric protected the
diner's clothing – still an important consideration today, when
guests are all dressed up in their finery. Provide a few spare
napkins in case of accidents, particularly for a buffet meal.

RIGHT Sets of monogrammed linen were once
painstakingly stitched by brides-to-be as part of
their trousseau. If you have the skill and the time,
you could sew initials on your own napkins.
Alternatively, if you're feeling extravagant,
commission a monogram from a commercial
machine embroiderer.

BELOW LEFT The unassuming elegance of
white-on-white embroidery speaks for itself and
needs little in the way of further embellishment.

BELOW CENTRE A special decorative touch for
the top table, maybe – sew a sprinkling of tiny
ribbon flowers to one corner of a white napkin
and display it in a wineglass.

BELOW RIGHT A border of buttonhole hemstitch
adds colour to a plain napkin, echoing the blue
edging on the flower-sprigged plate and saucer.

PROJECT 4
heart-shaped napkin tags

Napkins are the finishing touch to
a celebratory table laden with china,
flowers and sparking glassware. This
simple project sees napkins secured
with narrow ribbon and a handmade
heart-shaped tag that has been
decorated with vintage buttons or a
delicate lace effect. The pretty tags also
double up as wedding favours. They are
made from air-drying clay, which dries
to soft grey-white, but the tags could be
painted with acrylic craft paints to match
your wedding colour scheme.

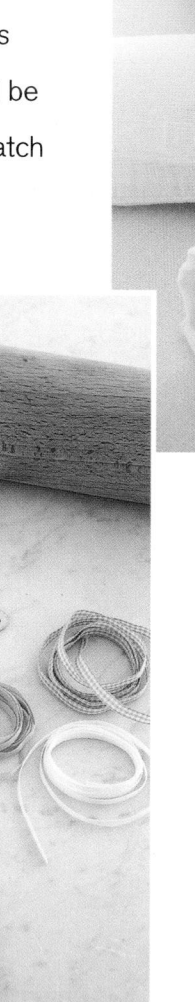

MATERIALS & EQUIPMENT
Air-drying or oven-hardening modelling clay
Rolling pin • Pastry board
Scraps of textured lace • Heart-shaped biscuit cutter
Selection of old buttons • Small leaves
Tapestry needle
Baking parchment • Cake rack
Fine sandpaper
40cm length of ribbon for each heart

1 Roll out some of the clay on the pastry board to a thickness of around 5mm. Position the lace over the top and press it down gently with the rolling pin. Peel back the lace to reveal the texture and cut out heart shapes with the cutter.

2 Roll out the remaining clay and cut more hearts. Carefully press one or two buttons or a small leaf into the middle of each one. Using the needle, pierce a hole, just big enough for the ribbon to go through, at the centre top.

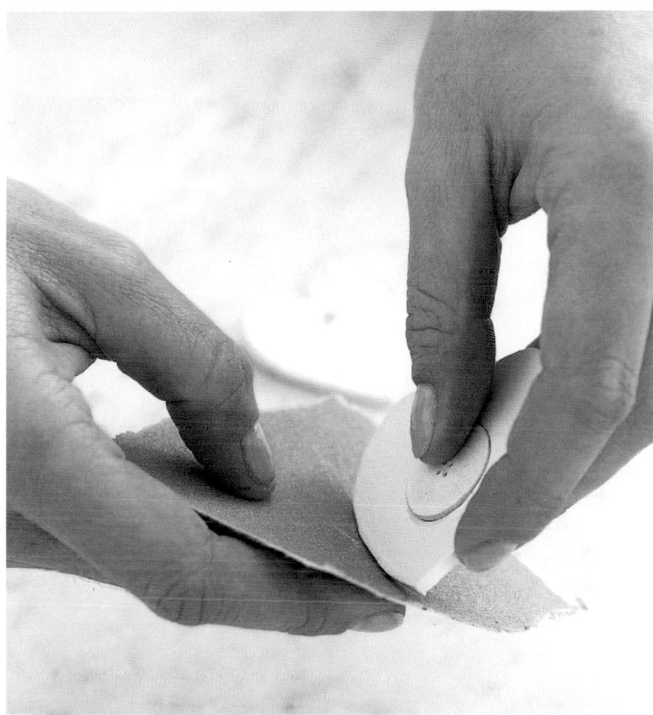

3 Lift up the hearts carefully and place them on a sheet of baking parchment. Let them dry or bake them in the oven if necessary, following the manufacturer's instructions. Once dry or cool, smooth any rough edges with sandpaper.

4 Thread a length of ribbon through each of the finished hearts. Fold a napkin in half and roll it up tightly lengthways. Tie the ribbon around the middle of the napkin and keep it in place by making the ends into a small bow.

heart-shaped napkin tags 51

ABOVE LEFT A small rectangular place card has been fixed to each of these cosmos daisies with a twist of florist's wire. The flowers have been placed in shot glasses and arranged in neat rows for easy identification.

ABOVE RIGHT Gold butterflies clip hand-finished paper leaves to an ivy garland. If, like this, your seating plan is to be hung up, allow room for your guests to gather around it.

place cards

A carefully thought-out seating plan is essential to the smooth running of any formal sit-down meal, but trying to work out the logistics of who should sit where can prove unexpectedly complicated. Give members of both families the opportunity to get to know each other, but remember that work colleagues, old friends and distant relatives may prefer to sit with each other.

To help your guests find their seats, you will need to display a seating plan – a list pinned to the wall or a framed chart on an easel. If you want something different, opt for small envelopes bearing the name of each guest with their table number written

LEFT Tie a place card to a spoon, all ready for afternoon tea or after-dinner coffee. The cups and saucers can be placed on the dining tables or arranged on a side table for after the meal.

OPPOSITE Serried ranks of cute white baby squashes add laid-back country style to an autumn wedding. Tiny slits have been made in each stalk to hold the hand-written place cards.

ABOVE A foretaste of the feasting to come: a computer-printed name card is tied to spears of asparagus and balanced atop a wineglass at each place.

ABOVE RIGHT Place-card holders are found in many stationers or gift shops and can double up as favours. This porcelain bunny is an unforgettable keepsake.

BELOW RIGHT Classic white tent-fold cards such as this one are available from stationers. If you want to jazz them up, try using coloured ink to write the names.

on a card inside. These can look extremely stylish when arranged in neat symmetrical rows on a table top.

At each setting, you'll need to display a place card. The traditional choice is a simple white card, but if you prefer, have fun with pastel shades or bold colours that tie in with your wedding colour scheme. If you have attractive handwriting, you could write the cards yourself. Alternatively, consider commisioning a calligrapher to pen the cards. Nowadays computers have a good choice of fonts, and their printouts are quick, cheap and easy to correct. You can even use the same font for the menus.

ABOVE LEFT Labelled wedding favours can double up as place cards. Here, enticing little favour boxes are tied with gold ribbon to match the plates and positioned at each setting.

TOP RIGHT Vivid redcurrants in white cake cases make a striking visual statement. Tuck the name labels in among the berries.

ABOVE RIGHT Understatedly elegant, a hand-written name card is tucked inside an exquisite embossed teacup at each setting.

PROJECT 5
pebble place cards

These smooth, matt pebbles with a pleasing chalky texture make a novel alternative to the traditional place card (the pebbles can be found at garden centres or ordered from florists). Each guest's name and table number is added to a pebble, then they can be arranged on large trays or platters, either arranged alphabetically or by table. Guests can then find their own pebble as they enter the reception room. If you are short of time, you can speed up the manufacturing process by buying wire that comes ready-threaded with glass beads.

MATERIALS & EQUIPMENT
Medium-sized white pebbles
Flexible medium-gauge dark-coloured wire
Wire cutters • Stick-on dots • Buttons
Sheet of rub-down letters and numbers • Pencil
Fine wire, such as floristry wire
Crystal beads, around 25 for each pebble
Small parcel labels or heart-shaped tags
3mm-wide satin ribbon
Tiny silk flowers

1   Cut a length of wire, approximately 60cm long, and attach one end to the underside of a pebble with an adhesive dot.

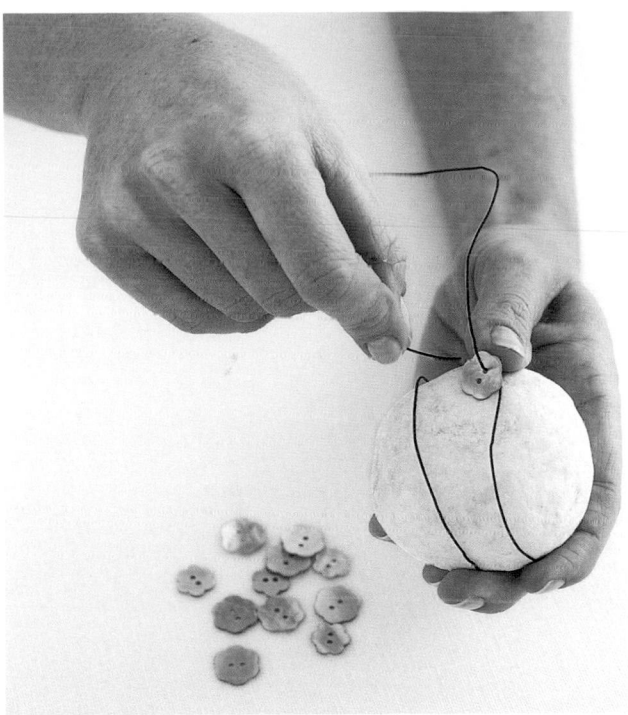

2 Wrap the wire once around the pebble and then thread it through one of the decorative buttons. Take it back round the pebble once more, trim the end, and anchor it to the underside using another adhesive dot.

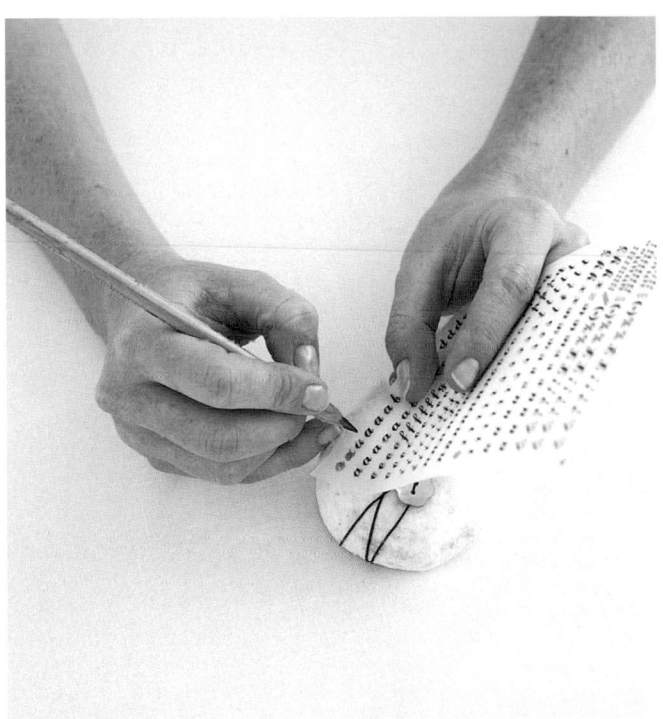

3 Rub down the letters of your chosen name centrally on to the pebble, taking care to space them evenly. Following the seating plan carefully, add the guest's table number to the pebble on the other side of the wire.

4 Alternatively, secure a 60cm length of fine wire to a pebble as before and thread on about 25 crystal beads. Wrap the wire around the pebble, sliding the beads to the top, and fix the end to the underside with an adhesive dot.

5 Write the guest's name on one small tag and his or her table number on another, either by hand or with rub-down letters. Thread the tags on a length of ribbon and tie it around the pebble. Finish off by tucking two silk flowers under the wire.

centrepieces

Table centrepieces don't have to consist of the traditional floral arrangements. An imaginative or quirky arrangement will prove a good conversation starter as your guests are seated. Many-tiered cake stands, glass compotes and old-fashioned etageres with two or three levels were all designed for display and look impressive when bedecked with fruit, bonbons, cakes or cookies. If you're sticking to a tight budget, you could even forgo expensive floral arrangements in favour of a cake stand holding biscuits or petits fours for guests to enjoy with their coffee.

ABOVE LEFT Roll firm, fresh fruit in beaten egg white and then in caster sugar to give it a frosted finish, but warn your guests that it is purely decorative, and not to be eaten!

LEFT Metallic craft paint has been used to write the table number on one of the blown glass baubles piled on this glass stand. Bunches of fresh grapes set amongst them add a slightly Bacchanalian air to the festivities.

RIGHT Sitting like a swan in a sea of sugared almonds, this table number is made from silver beads threaded onto pliable wire and bent gently into a '2' shape. Its height makes it easy to identify from a distance.

FAR RIGHT A tiered cake stand can be set in the middle of the table to allow guests to reach out for hand-made chocolate truffles to accompany cups of after-dinner coffee.

An imaginative or quirky arrangement will prove a good conversation starter.

RIGHT These sugared almonds in a Victorian fluted compote tie in to a sophisticated silver and white colour scheme.

FAR RIGHT Dainty decorated biscuits are arranged on a tiered glass cake stand. The enticing goodies can be enjoyed with tea or coffee after dinner has ended.

PROJECT 6
chair cover

An ordinary wooden dining chair can be transformed into something special by concealing it with this simple slip cover, made from a combination of plain linen and pretty faded chintz. Sew a chair cover both for the bride and groom, and decorate them with either their initials or a monogram embroidered on the back. You do not need to be an experienced upholsterer to make this project, so don't be deterred by its professional appearance: the cover is not fitted to the chair and, since the linen drapes softly over the seat, there are no curved seams.

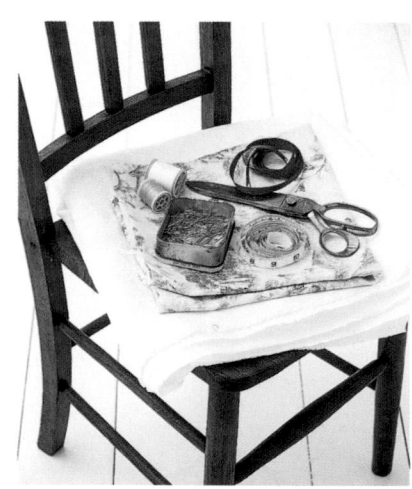

MATERIALS & EQUIPMENT
Tape measure • Scissors • Ruler and pencil
Squared pattern paper
50cm square of flowered fabric
150 x 50cm white linen or cotton fabric
Sewing machine
Coloured sewing thread or embroidery thread
Dressmaker's pins • Sewing needle
Matching sewing thread
2m of 15mm-wide satin ribbon to match flowered fabric

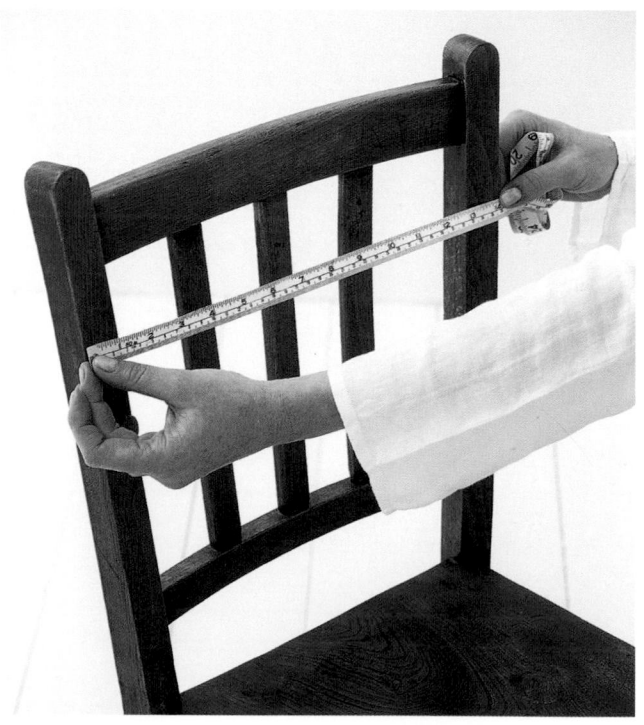

1   Measure up the chair. Add a 4cm seam allowance to each panel. You need a panel for the back, one for the front, two side and one front skirt panels, and the seat. Add 5cm to the back and front panels for the depth of the chair back.

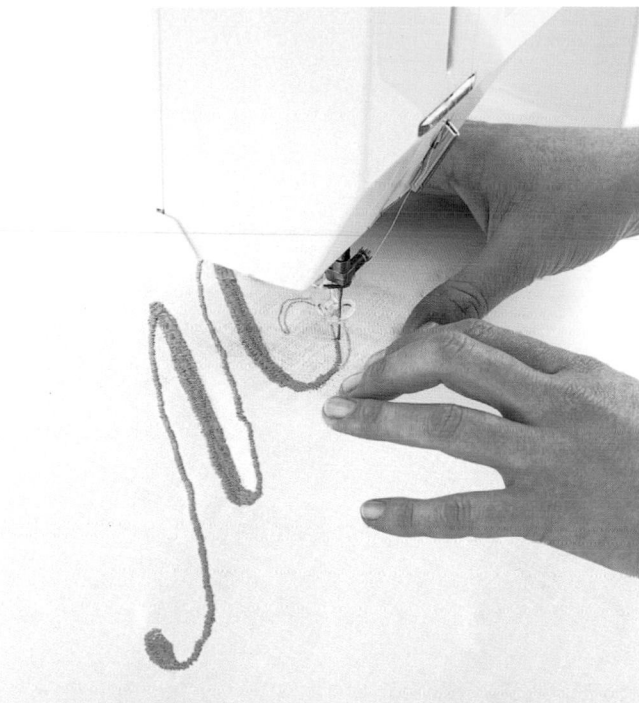

2 Transfer the measurements to the pattern paper and cut out the templates, labelling each one. Check the sizes against the chair and adjust as necessary. Cut out the chair seat from flowered fabric and the other pieces from plain linen.

3 Trace the outline of your chosen monogram on the front panel and embroider the letter by hand or machine. Fit an embroidery foot if you have one and work in satin stitch in a colour to match the floral fabric.

4 With right sides together, pin the front and back panels together and slip over the chair. Pin on the seat and the skirt to check the fit. Hem along the sides and bottom of the skirt panels and the lower part of the back.

5 Leaving 2cm seams, sew the side and front skirts to the seat. Stitch the seat to the lower edge of the front panel. Sew the long back to the front, turn inside out, and press. Make four ribbon bows and stitch to each corner of the seat.

Candles

The flickering flames and soft shadows of candlelight
add an air of enchantment and intimacy to any event,
thus making it the perfect addition to your wedding party.
Whether you opt for classic many-branched candelabra,
tall ivory-hued pillars, slender tapers or simple tealights in
jam jars, the tiny flames, with their warmth and romantic
glow, will inevitably cast their spell over your guests.

ABOVE LEFT A simple centrepiece is created by a cream pillar candle on a fluted cake stand, surrounded by a handful of rose petals and fragrant white jasmine flowers.

ABOVE RIGHT This eclectic gathering of pressed-glass tumblers and engraved wineglasses reflects the soft light cast by the candles. Twist crystal beads on to silver craft wire to make sparkling garlands like those that surround the pillar and votive candles.

The romantic atmosphere created by candles will enhance any reception, whether it is held indoors or outside, and whatever the surroundings. Silver candelabra can be found at the middle of traditional table arrangements, while individual votives at each place setting are less formal. Groups of candles always look stunning, and can be set on side tables, used as centrepieces or arranged on mantelpieces or windowsills. A word of warning, however: lighted candles must be placed out of harm's way and should never be left unattended.

LEFT Larger candles, which have two or more wicks to ensure even burning, make bright focal points for centrepieces like this garland of ivy and leaf-shaped name cards.

ABOVE A handful of tapers emerge from a froth of cow parsley and white nerines. The tapers are inserted into a block of wet florist's foam, which holds them securely in place.

BELOW Bowls of floating candles make eye-catching centrepieces. Pale pink candles have been chosen to complement the red roses and blush-coloured petals that float alongside.

RIGHT Single lily heads drift alongside lighted white candles in a simple porcelain bowl. They create an ethereal feeling of calm and tranquillity within an all-white table scheme.

BELOW This smaller group features just three candles, set amidst scattered rose petals. The soft glow of the flames casts patterned shadows through the glass bowl and on to the tablecloth below.

ABOVE RIGHT Arranging a multitude of candles on a reflective surface – a mirror or polished silver tray – will double their impact. Faceted or embossed glass tealight holders, like these ones, add to the glittering effect.

RIGHT Create a sense of height by using tall candles, or by arranging votive candles on a tiered cake stand. Used singly, these ribbed, frosted glass votive holders are pretty, but when many are grouped together the overall effect is spectacular. The paper-lace doily, reminiscent of afternoon tea, is a delicate finishing touch.

ABOVE LEFT Turn an ordinary beaded votive
holder into a hanging lantern by tying both ends
of a length of ribbon to the top rim. These
bejewelled versions are suspended from the
canopy of a weeping willow.

ABOVE RIGHT Suspended in mid air, these
delicate blown glass globes look like soap
bubbles floating serenely past. Always make
sure that candles are firmly secured within their
holders by using special pliable wax or a blob
of molten wax from a lit candle.

LEFT Light your guests' way with a row
of candles, placed at intervals along a path
or terrace. These votive holders have been
decorated with evergreen leaves and berries.

ABOVE LEFT The lace-like dome and panels of this pierced-tin lantern are specially intended to cast decorative shadows. Look out for similar Moroccan-style lights at shops that specialize in similar ethnic accessories.

ABOVE CENTRE Chandelier-like crystal drops dangle from this decorative wirework votive holder. For a summer wedding out of doors, dot a series of lanterns around the garden for your guests to discover as twilight falls.

ABOVE RIGHT White rice (a suitably bridal choice) has been used to fill a stout glass vase and support a pillar candle. Dishwasher salt or glass pebbles are good alternatives. A tall-sided vase or hurricane lantern is a sensible choice for an outdoor venue, as the glass will protect both the flame and your guests from mishaps.

LEFT A row of concertina lanterns illuminates a garlanded arbour late into the night, creating the perfect setting for a summer party.

candles 69

PROJECT 7
jam-jar candleholders

With a little glitter and glue, glass jam and food jars can easily be transformed into glamorous, sparkly tealight holders. Collect a variety of differently sized jars, then decorate them with a scattering of glitter, beads and diamantés in delicate toning colours. The candleholders look fabulous arranged in clusters, in a row along the mantelpiece or positioned singly on each table in the reception room. Do remember to be safety-conscious – never leave a burning candle unattended.

MATERIALS & EQUIPMENT
Jam jars in a range of different sizes
Assortment of glass beads
Fine wire • Wire cutters
PVA adhesive • Tweezers
Stick-on diamantés
Glitter • Saucer • Tealights

1. Wrap one end of a 75cm length of wire once around the rim of the jar and secure. Thread on about 50 beads and spiral the wire along the ridges of the screw top, spacing out the beads. Twist and clip the ends of the wire.

2. Decorate the jar with a sprinkling of diamantés. Apply a tiny dab of glue to the back of a diamanté and leave it until nearly dry. Pick up a stone with tweezers or press it on to the tip of your finger, then push it firmly on to the glass.

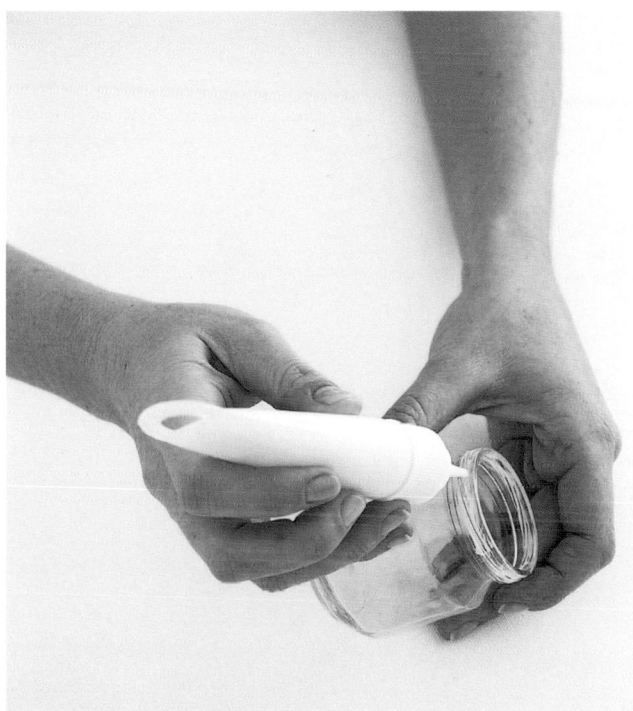

3. For an alternative effect, decorate the rims of the jars with glitter. Apply an even coating of glue all around the outside of the screw top and allow to dry slightly.

4. Tip the glitter into a saucer, then dip the jar in the glitter so that the glue is completely covered all over. Leave until the glue is quite dry. If the coating is not even, add glue to the patchy areas and dip the jar again until the rim is concealed.

Wedding favours

The custom of presenting wedding guests with favours — small keepsakes or delicious edible treats in gorgeous wrappings — is a long-established and popular tradition. Whether you place a pretty package at each table setting to make everybody feel personally welcome, or distribute them as parting gifts as your guests leave the reception, these charming little gifts act as gracious tokens of thanks, appreciation and mutual celebration.

LEFT Sugar-frosted amaretti, an Italian favourite, go perfectly with after-dinner drinks. Here they have been packaged in a simple Cellophane bag with a knot of blue ribbon, placed in cups and saucers, then set out in rows on a side table. Tiny macaroons, biscotti or gingerbread biscuits could be presented in a similar way.

BELOW Part of a gold and white setting, these foil-covered chocolate hearts look sophisticated in a gold-rimmed champagne glass.

edible favours

Sweet favours are always popular. Silvered or pastel sugared almonds are the traditional wedding choice, but individually wrapped crystallized fruit, truffles or colourful sweets are all excellent alternatives. Their packaging need not be elaborate or expensive: iced biscuits or foil-wrapped sweets can be clad in tissue paper or Cellophane and tied with satin or paper ribbon. While other favours are intended as souvenirs, these mouth-watering treats are offered as an accompaniment to coffee and liqueurs at the end of the meal – if your guests can wait!

LEFT If time is at a premium (and your budget allows), search for a specialist manufacturer who can supply ready-packaged sweets, like this charmingly old-fashioned box of chocolate rose creams. You can then add a personal touch with ribbon, silk flowers or a paper lace doily to fit in with the rest of your table setting.

BELOW Coloured icing and a fine nozzle were used to pipe names on to these rectangular biscuits, giving them an extra role as edible place cards. They have been arranged around a table number made from blue glass beads threaded on to florist's wire and bent into a '5'. Delicate bows to match the icing add the final touch.

Irresistible edible favours will add colour, flavour and fun to the reception table.

Guests of all ages will be delighted by these truly scrumptious treats.

FAR LEFT To save time, go for instant packaging. Fill clear plastic boxes with pastel-coloured sweets and tie them up with ribbon bows.

CENTRE LEFT Cellophane cones are filled with white jellybeans and tied with sage-green ribbon. Sugared almonds would work equally well.

LEFT Little bundles of sugared almonds have been presented to wedding guests for centuries, as tokens of thanks and good fortune. In Italy, brides wrap five almonds in net to symbolize the five qualities that contribute to a lasting and happy marriage: health, wealth, fertility, happiness and long life.

LEFT Three variations on a pink and white theme prove the versatility of edible favours: a bag of gold hearts wrapped in Cellophane is tied with a gauzy bow, while white almonds look good in a tissue-lined box or tied up with a polka dot ribbon.

ABOVE LEFT Tempting pink truffles are too pretty to hide away in a box.

ABOVE RIGHT AND TOP
On a more fanciful note, at a late summer wedding a whimsical arrangement of beribboned baby pumpkins looks good enough to eat!

RIGHT Fine green ribbon, in a shade
that exactly matches the enchanting fresh
rosebuds, is used to tie up these white gift
boxes and to secure the name tags. Make
sure that the buds are added at the very last
minute, so that they do not wilt.

BELOW LEFT Bundles of slender hand-
dipped candles make a lasting memento that
need no further adornment than a simple
silver-grey cord tie.

BELOW RIGHT Subtly wrapped packages
will intrigue your guests. These transparent
glassine envelopes contain fine scented
soaps, but could equally well be used to
package a sachet of dried lavender, spicy
potpourri or a scented candle.

non-edible favours

The content of these pretty packages will depend very much on your budget and personal taste. Favours do not have to be expensive (particularly if you have a lot of guests), so use your imagination and have fun selecting something to please your friends and family. A packet of seeds or a bulb in a miniature terracotta pot, a hand-written verse or a tealight holder are good for those on a tight budget. Other ingenious ideas include a CD of the music played during the service, a slim volume of poetry or a scented candle.

ABOVE LEFT Bright ribbons bring colour to a stack of square boxes. Choose stripes, checks, velvet and ombré ribbons in matching shades

ABOVE RIGHT AND RIGHT
Fill envelopes with flower seeds, add a card with planting instructions and tie with a matching bow of ribbon.

ABOVE Keeping to shades of just one colour will always create a glamorous, grown-up effect. Here, a sheer burgundy ribbon has been used to tie a pale pink rose to a deeper pink favour box.

ABOVE RIGHT This picot-edged braid was carefully chosen to enhance the shade of the engraved blue wineglass. A place card has been slipped under the bow so that the place setting is easy to locate.

RIGHT Another single-colour favour, this time in ethereal shades of cream: a silk flower corsage in a translucent onyx bowl adds a romantic and dreamy atmosphere to the dining table.

INSET RIGHT Twist faceted crystals on to fine craft wire to create a pliable garland to wrap round a packaged favour. Clear and green glass beads threaded on silver wire have been used to carry through the green and pink colour scheme of this wedding reception.

ABOVE LEFT AND CENTRE A dainty, decorative handkerchief makes an unusual substitute for wrapping paper, and is a lasting favour in itself. Look out for lawn square or Irish linen with hemstitched borders or flower-sprigged embroidery. Place a small favour in the centre, then gather the corners together with a velvet bow or twist of wire disguised with a silk flower.

ABOVE RIGHT A couple with a shared love of gardening might opt for a miniature galvanized bucket filled with grape hyacinths and accessorized with a flower-fairy-sized fork. Once planted outside, these will come up year after year as a reminder of a happy occasion.

LEFT Nowadays, artificial fabric flowers are almost indistinguishable from the real thing. To adorn an extravagant gold-coloured favour box, choose a decorative bloom that matches the bride's bouquet or the table flowers .

non-edible favours 81

PROJECT 8
lavender hearts

These dainty lavender bag favours are guaranteed to enchant your guests. They are a special keepsake, and the evocative scent of the lavender that fills them will remind guests of your wedding day. If you prefer, you could fill the hearts with potpourri, dried rosebuds, or other fragrant petals: the muted colour of the flowers will show prettily through the delicate organza. The hearts are decorated with simple embroidery and felt flowers, circles of Indian shisha mirror glass and sequins, and finished off with a hanging loop of narrow braid.

MATERIALS & EQUIPMENT
For each heart:
15 x 30cm rectangle of sheer or opaque silk fabric
Tracing paper and pencil • Dressmaker's pins
Scissors • Pink and green felt
Stranded embroidery cotton • Embroidery needle
Flower-shaped sequins • Pink and green sewing thread
30cm of narrow braid • PVA adhesive
Stick-on diamantés • Shisha mirrors • Lavender

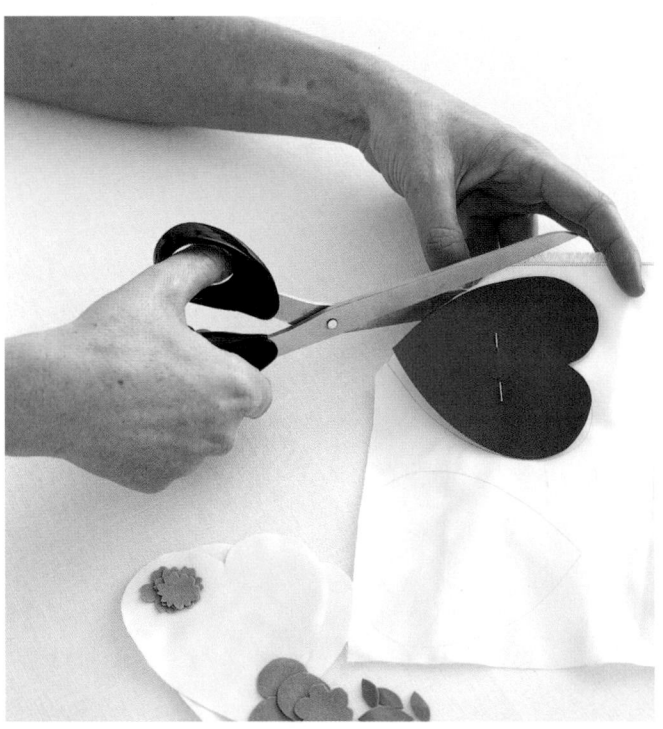

1 Trace off the heart and flower templates on page 111. Use them as a guide to cut out two hearts from silk fabric and three pink felt flowers. Snip out six green felt leaf shapes.

2 Thread a large-eyed needle with all six strands of a length of embroidery cotton. Work a line of small, regular running stitches around the edge of one fabric heart, with a spiral at each end. This will be the front piece of the bag.

3 Arrange and pin the leaves and flowers to the front piece as shown. Anchor the flowers with flower-shaped sequins: work six straight stitches from the hole to the outside edge. Sew the leaves along the centre spine with back stitch.

4 Fold the braid in half. Pin the two ends to the top of the front heart on the wrong side, then pin the back heart in place. Sew together around the outside edge, leaving a 4cm open gap. Fill the bag with lavender, then sew up the gap.

5 Glue a diamanté close to the flowers with PVA adhesive. Make further bags in the same way, varying them by using sheer fabric, different braid or adding darker flower centres and gluing on shisha mirrors alongside the diamantés.

Finishing touches

Spend time and thought on planning the finishing touches for your wedding: it is these tiny details that will make the day unique. Here you'll find a wealth of beautiful ideas, ranging from confetti (to add a romantic touch to proceedings) to suggestions for thoughtful thank-you gifts that will delight your attendants. There's even a project for a hand-stitched ring pillow that will become an instant family heirloom.

confetti

As they cast handfuls of confetti over a newly married couple, wedding guests are unconsciously partaking in a ritual that dates back centuries. Today's bride and groom are likely to be showered with flower petals or delicate paper cutouts of hearts and horseshoes, but pagan couples were bombarded with rice or nuts, in the belief that the fertile seeds would ensure a prolific marriage. At a later date, these grains would be coated in sugar crystals and became known by the Italian term *confetti*, meaning 'sweetmeats'. Do check whether your wedding venue welcomes paper confetti. Many no longer do, but dried or fresh rose and delphinium petals or even dried hops are an attractive biodegradable alternative, while the latest trend of blowing soap bubbles is exuberant, fun and leaves no mess behind.

TOP LEFT At the exit from the ceremony, place a few simple wooden baskets filled with rice to encourage wedding guests to take part in an ancient tradition.

TOP CENTRE Prepare fresh rose petals at the last minute so that they retain their scent and shape. Hold a rose head in one hand, then twist and pull the stem gently with the other, so that the bloom falls apart.

CENTRE These tiny white petals will fall in a snow-like flurry.

BOTTOM LEFT Pure white daisy shapes are an attractive minimalist alternative to the multicoloured pastels typical of most paper confetti.

TOP RIGHT Choose a pretty basket with an easy-to-hold handle for the littlest bridesmaids or flower girls.

BOTTOM RIGHT An enamel bucket makes a more utilitarian container, but one that has its own quirky charm and is ideal for a simple country wedding. This one is filled with a combination of fragrant jasmine and rose petals.

A shower of confetti is a joyful symbol
of both fruitfulness and festivity.

ABOVE LEFT Simple white cartons can be
bought from wedding or stationery suppliers.
Simply fill them up with fresh petals, close the
lid and tie a gauzy ribbon around each one.

ABOVE CENTRE These origami-style folded
paper parcels are filled with rice and tied with
raffia knots. They are arranged on a bamboo
tray, ready to be distributed after the service:
a useful task for a young attendant to perform.

ABOVE RIGHT AND INSET OPPOSITE RIGHT
To form a confetti cone, fold over two sides of
a hand-made paper square. Secure the edges
with paper glue or double-sided tape, then fill
the cone with pieces of torn paper and fabric
or real flower petals. Make one cone for each
guest and present them all massed together
in a wicker basket.

RIGHT These dainty linen drawstring bags are
for the bride's attendants. Fill them with confetti
and hand them out before the ceremony.

TOP RIGHT Pearly grains of rice represent fertility and good fortune. Throwing them (gently!) at the bride and groom after the wedding ceremony is an ancient rite.

LEFT Embroidered sprays of lily of the valley decorate these confetti bags. Make them from a square of fine cotton, seamed at the side and bottom edges, then hemmed at the top and tied with a length of pretty ribbon.

gifts for attendants

Whatever the age of your bridesmaids, flower girls or ring bearers, and whatever their role on the day, all your attendants deserve a special thank-you gift. Select each present carefully, finding something to match each person's tastes, then wrap them beautifully. Indulgent treats for your girlfriends might include a silver photo frame, a dainty evening bag, a bottle of their favourite perfume or a charm bracelet. Younger attendants will be thrilled with a special story book, a toy or even a 'grown-up' watch or small piece of jewellery.

BELOW Recreate this look by binding a box with a wide lilac ribbon, then tying longer lengths of gauze and satin ribbons over it and finishing with a bow. A velvet flower is the final flourish.

TOP RIGHT Variations on a theme: these sumptuous silk confetti bags make lasting souvenirs for bridesmaids or flower girls. Each one is embroidered with flowers or leaves, and has a cord drawstring closure.

RIGHT Create this luxurious evening bag by folding a strip of brocade in half and seaming the side edges. Trim the top with marabou and tie it up with satin ribbon. Add another loop of ribbon so it can be hung from the wrist.

OPPOSITE, MAIN PICTURE Gift-wrapping does not have to be elaborate to be effective: here, crisp striped ribbons add a touch of drama to these small attendants' gift boxes.

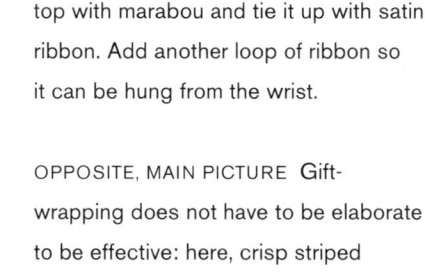

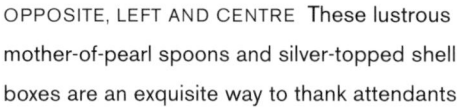

OPPOSITE, LEFT AND CENTRE These lustrous mother-of-pearl spoons and silver-topped shell boxes are an exquisite way to thank attendants.

OPPOSITE, RIGHT Metallic ribbons give a sophisticated finish to a gift. Fix each length to the underside with sticky tape or a glue stick.

PROJECT 9
bridesmaid's bag

These pretty bridesmaids' bags are easy to make and require only basic sewing skills. Their quirky charm comes from the numerous ribbons, buttons and beads with which they are embellished. To achieve a similar vintage look, scour flea markets or ask your friends and relations to turn out their sewing baskets and donate any suitable trimmings. Use a piece of linen or remnants of the bridesmaids' dress fabric for the bags and, for real individuality, make each one very slightly different.

MATERIALS & EQUIPMENT
Pieces of silk or similar fabric
Long ruler and dressmaker's chalk • Pinking shears
Iron • Stranded embroidery thread
Embroidery needle
Matching and contrasting sewing thread
Selection of pearl buttons and sequins
Dressmaker's pins • Sewing machine (optional)
45cm length of medium-width ribbon or lace
Scraps of paper silk • Brooch backing
40cm of narrow ribbon

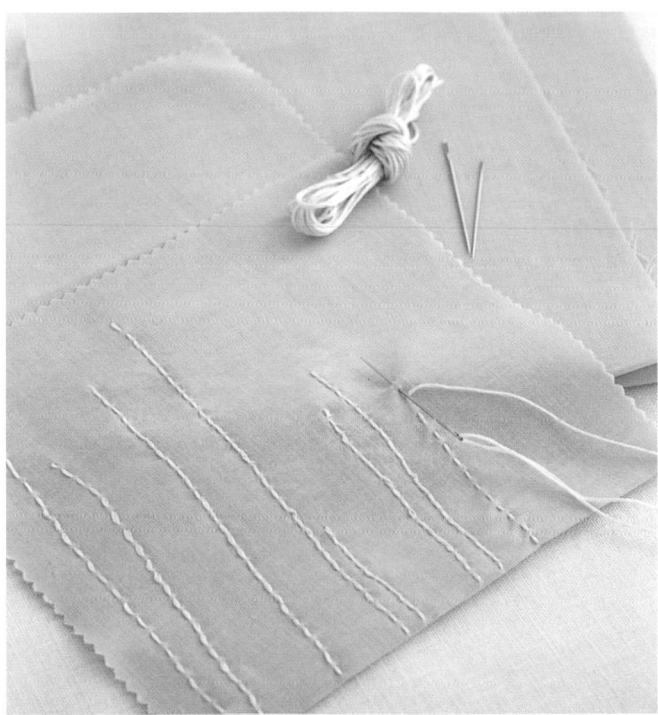

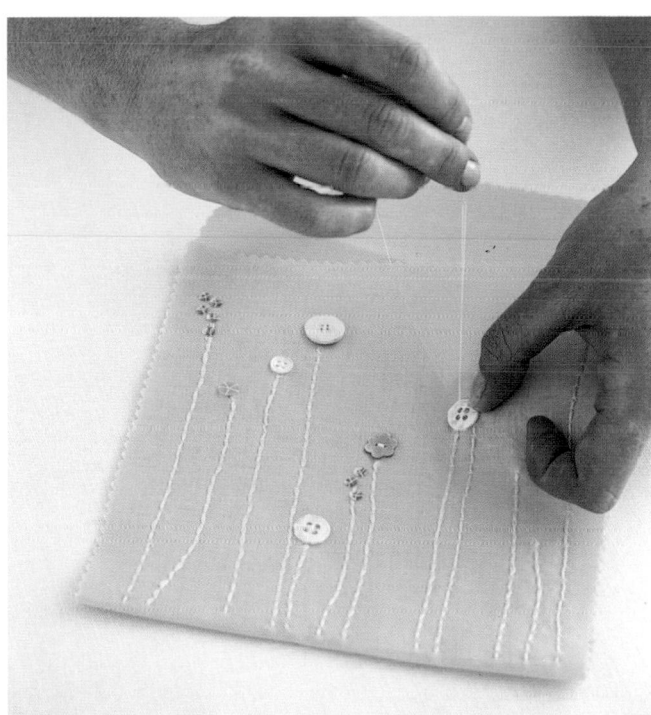

1 Using pinking shears, cut a 18 x 48cm piece of fabric. Press under a 6cm turning at one short end to make a flap, then fold the other short end up to the crease and press. Sew vertical lines of running stitch up the front of the bag.

2 Sew one or more sequins above four of the running-stitch stalks to make a flower head. Stitch from the centre to the rim in a star pattern. Pick out eight buttons in various sizes and hand-stitch them to the top of the remaining stalks.

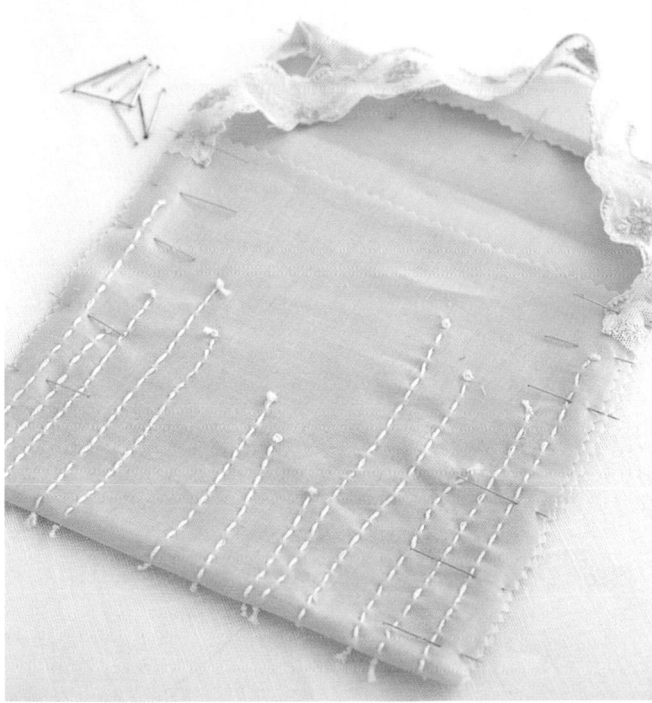

3 With wrong sides facing, pin the edges of the bag together. Pin one end of the lace or ribbon to each top corner, then stitch the seams, making sure the handle is secured. Hem the flap. Turn the bag right side out and press.

4 Cut four different-sized flower shapes from the silk, using the template on page 111. Stack them together and stitch through the centre. Stitch the flower to the brooch backing. Make bows from the narrow ribbon and sew to the corners.

RIGHT If you want to move away from a pale palette, go for taupe, which is always a good neutral background colour and looks great with gold.

FAR RIGHT The satin top of this ivory bag is trimmed with insertion lace through which a fine cord has been threaded. An oriental bead provides a 'something old' fastening.

BELOW RIGHT A 20cm length of braid is all you need for an edging, so you could opt for something wildly extravagant that would otherwise be prohibitively expensive.

BELOW This plump pillow is covered in a tactile bouclé fabric with a subtle looped braid along two side seams.

ring bags and pillows

The exchange of rings is the pivotal moment of the wedding ceremony, and one which is charged with symbolism and emotion. Safeguarding the two precious wedding bands and delivering them into the hands of the bride and groom is usually the responsibility of the best man, although at some weddings he will entrust them to a young ring bearer clutching a pillow just before the ceremony starts. Make sure that the rings do not go astray, by safeguarding them in a tiny bag, which can sit safely in a pocket. If your gown has been made to measure, ask the dressmaker for an offcut from which to make the bag. Alternatively, look out for luxurious fabrics, such as transparent organza, plush velvet or pleated satin, and utilize pretty cords and ribbons for the drawstring.

THIS PAGE To make an unusual button into an eye-catching toggle, fold a 15cm length of cord in half and tie a loop 3cm from the centre. Sew the two loose ends to the back of the button, then slip the loop round the bag and over the button.

PROJECT 10
ring pillow

The heart-shaped pocket on the front of this dainty satin pillow will make it easy for even the youngest and most nervous ring bearer to perform the important task of looking after the two wedding bands. It will also alleviate the worries of the best man, as the rings are clearly visible at all times! Like the heart-shaped favours shown on page 82, this ring pillow is filled with dried lavender, so the evocative scent will fill the room as the rings are exchanged – the most important and moving moment in the wedding ceremony.

MATERIALS & EQUIPMENT
25 x 50cm piece of white satin
Dressmaker's pins • Sewing needle
Sewing machine (optional)
White sewing cotton • Scissors
15cm square of white organza • Red sewing cotton
Pearl button • 2cm heart cut from red felt
Small white bow • Sheet of paper
85cm of narrow decorative edging
Lavender

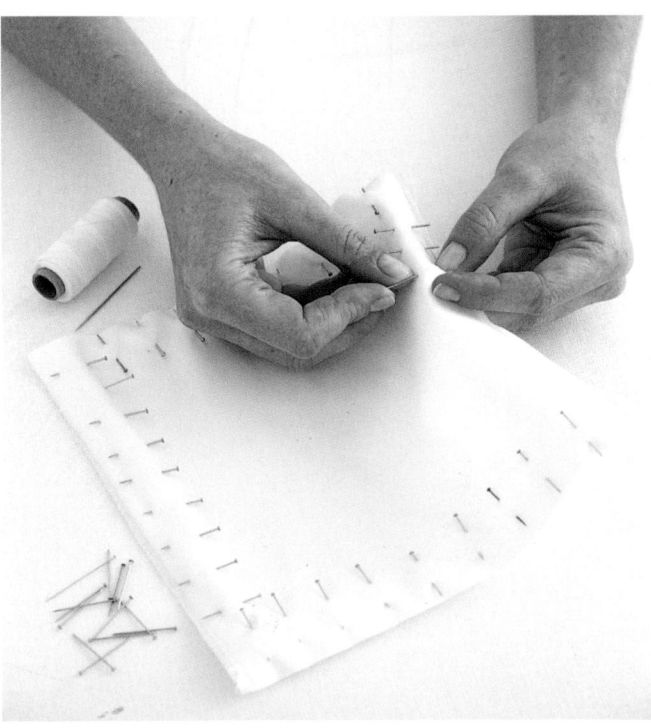

1   Cut two pieces of white satin, each 20 x 22cm. Place them together, right sides facing, and pin around all four edges. Machine- or hand-stitch 1cm from the edge, leaving a 4cm gap along one side. Turn right side out and press.

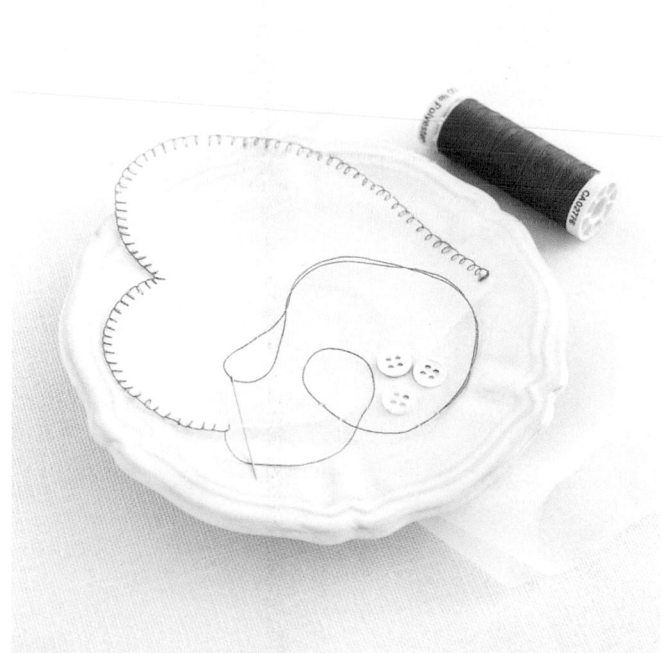

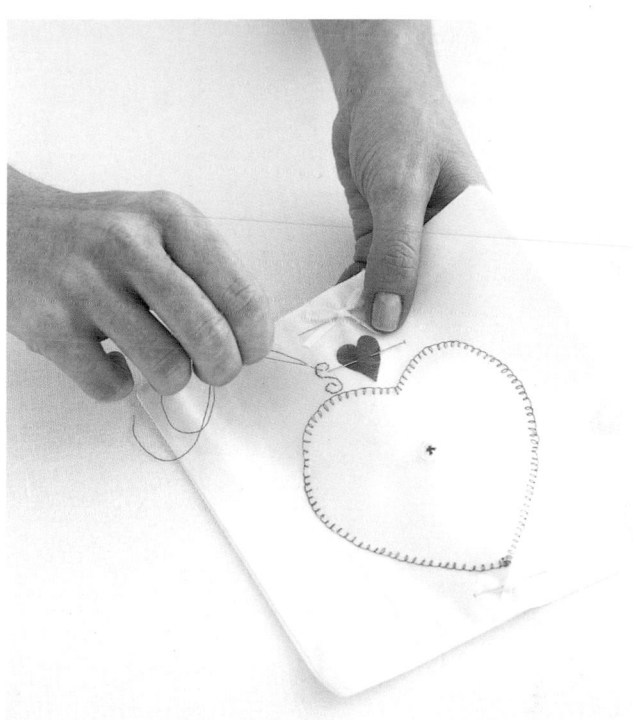

2 Cut a heart shape from the organza (using the template on page 111 if you wish). Thread a needle with a length of red sewing cotton and work a round of blanket stitch around the outside edge. Sew a button to the centre of the heart.

3 Pin the heart to the front of the pillow and sew in place with more blanket stitches, leaving the top edge open. Pin and stitch the heart and bow above the heart pocket. Embroider the bride's and groom's initials either side of the small heart.

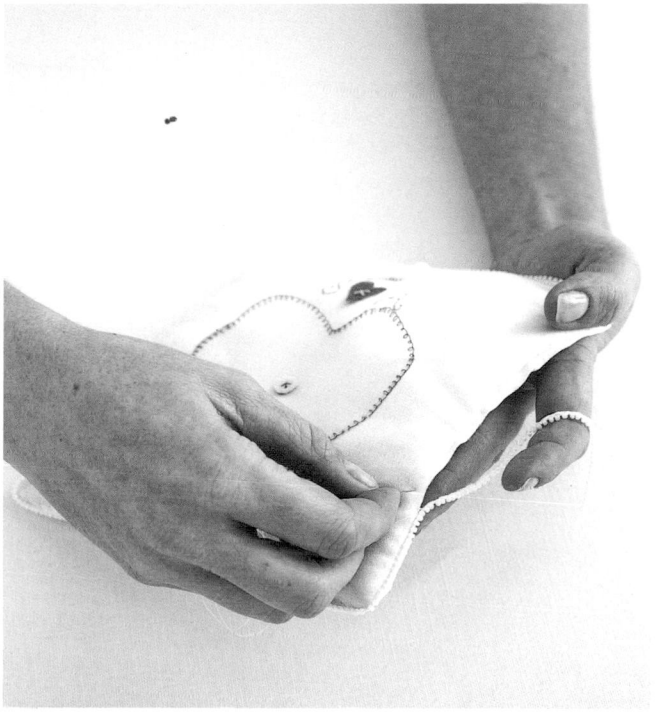

4 Fill the pillow with the dried lavender. You may find it helps to roll a sheet of paper into a cone, then insert the tip through the gap in the side seam and pour the lavender in through the top.

5 Neatly sew up the opening with small slip stitches. Finish off by hand-sewing the decorative trimming around all four sides of the pillow, again using small slip stitches worked in a matching sewing thread.

Keepsakes

Months of planning, weeks of anticipation, hopes, fears
and endless listmaking will all culminate in a whirlwind
of excitement when your wedding day finally arrives.
Make sure that you, your family and your friends
remember every joyous moment of the celebrations by
collecting together all the ephemera – snapshots, official
pictures, menu cards and messages – in specially made
photograph albums and guest books, and sending out
individual acknowledgments to each of your guests.

thank-you notes

It is a matter of politeness to send a card or letter to each of your guests on your return from honeymoon, or soon after the wedding, to thank them personally for attending the ceremony and to express your appreciation for the gifts they have given you. These notes should be hand-written, and taking the time to hand-make the cards is further proof of your gratitude for their kindness and good wishes.

ABOVE LEFT Interesting leaves adorn hand-made cards.

LEFT The edge of a doily makes a decorative mount for a white-bordered sepia photograph.

TOP RIGHT Print out small-scale versions of your favourite photo – a formal group or an off-guard moment caught by your best friend. Trim them down and fix to manilla card with traditional photo-corners.

ABOVE LEFT If you have the time, you can make each card to its own individual design, rather than mass-producing them.

ABOVE CENTRE A close-up photograph of your wedding bouquet is a wonderful image for a thank-you card. Black-and-white or sepia prints have a timeless air, and monochrome prints can always be made from coloured images.

ABOVE RIGHT Write your letters on sheets of beautifully textured hand-made rag paper, then roll them up and secure with a blob of coloured sealing wax. Stamp the wax with your new initial for a traditional finishing touch.

LEFT To make these understatedly elegant cards, fold a rectangle of deckle-edged hand-made paper in half and, using a scalpel, cut a square window in the centre front. Tie a length of ribbon in a bow close to the crease and glue a small souvenir – a fan of paper, a dried flower or a confetti petal – on the inside of the card, so it is clearly visible through the window.

PROJECT 11
guest book

Guest books are a relatively recent innovation at weddings, but they provide a lasting memento that will be treasured for years. They are also a wonderful way of giving friends and relations the opportunity to express their own thoughts and wishes for the bride and groom. Leave the book on a quiet table in the reception room or a side room, along with a pen, so that your guests will have time to sit, reflect and write a personal message. You may have to put up a small sign directing your guests to the book and asking everybody to make an entry.

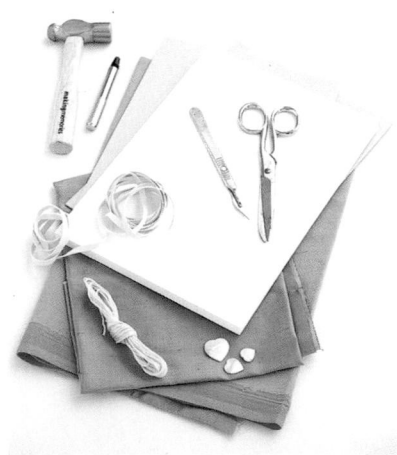

MATERIALS & EQUIPMENT
2 sheets of thick cardboard • Tape measure or long ruler
Pencil • Scissors • Fabric for cover
Contrasting fabric for lining
Embroidery needle • Stranded embroidery thread • Button
Double-sided adhesive tape • Stick-on dots
3m of narrow ribbon
2cm stack of paper, the same size as the card
Professional hole punch

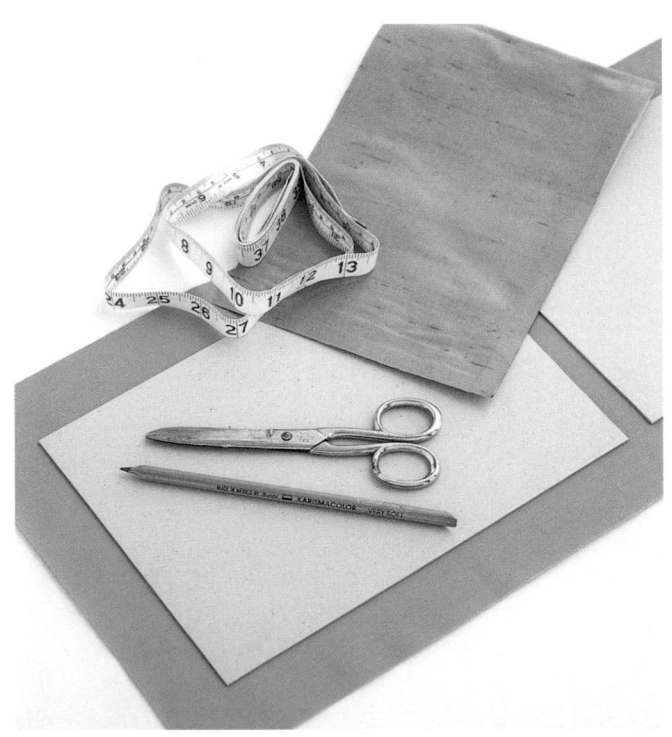

1   The fabric cover must be 8cm deeper than the card and twice its length plus 10cm. The lining is 2cm less than the depth and twice the length, plus 2cm. For size A4 you will need 29 x 70cm cover fabric and 18 x 62cm of lining.

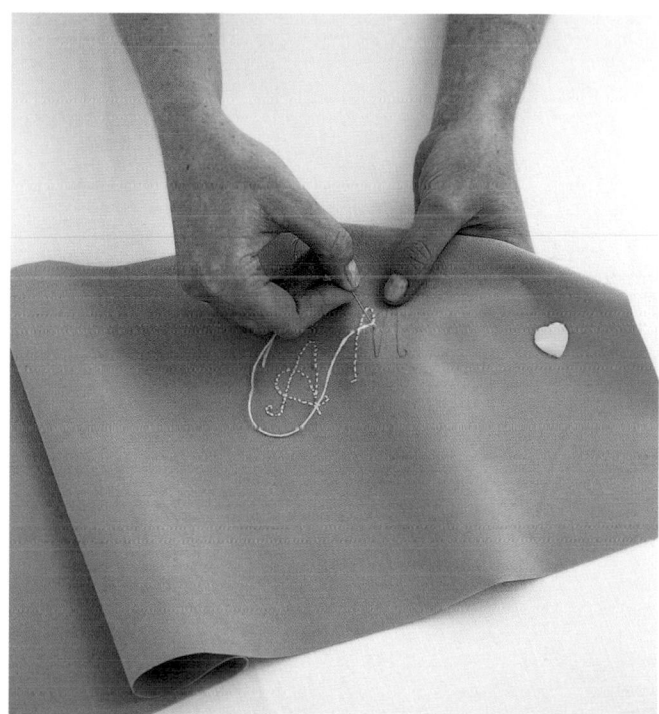

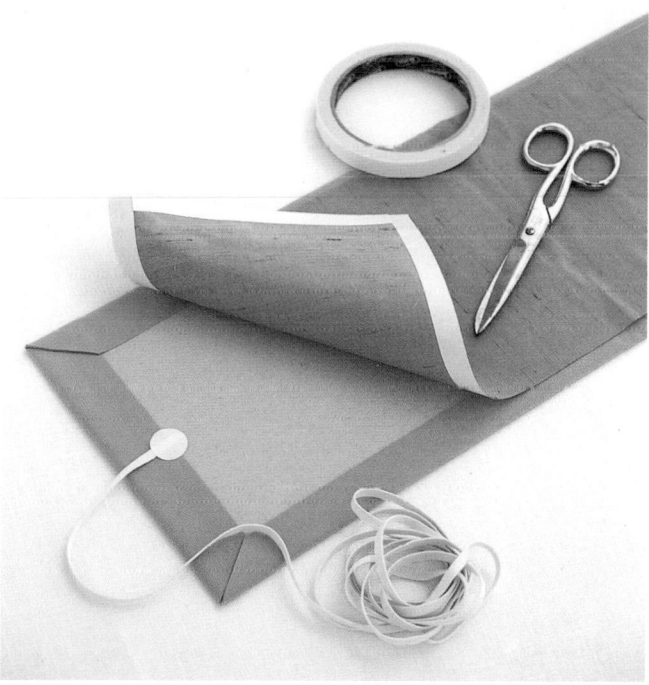

2   Mark the position for the initials on the front (leave 4cm for the turnings at the top and right edges), then draw them in. Sew over the lines in running stitch using the embroidery thread. Sew the button 5cm from the centre-right edge.

3   Tape the cover fabric to the pieces of card. Turn over 4cm at each edge and leave a 2cm gap between the boards for the spine. Mitre the corners. Fix 1m of ribbon to the front edge. Tape on the lining, leaving a 2cm margin all round.

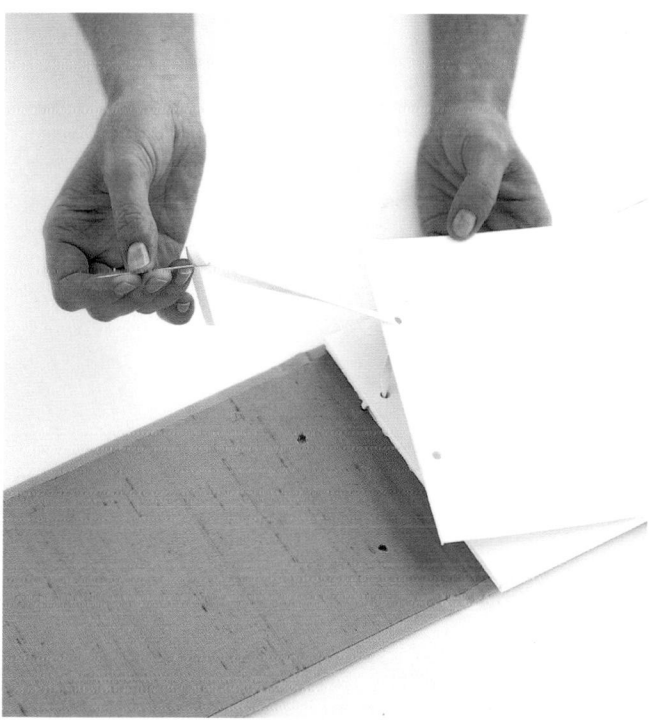

4   Punch two holes through the stack of paper, 15mm from one edge. Make two holes in corresponding positions on the front and back covers. Use an office punch for the paper and a bradawl to pierce the card.

5   Cut the remaining ribbon into two 50cm lengths. Thread them through the holes in the paper, then through the front and back covers. Tie loosely in position, so that the book can open easily, then finish off each ribbon with a bow.

ABOVE LEFT AND ABOVE A set
of matching albums, like these
beautiful hand-bound volumes,
will hold honeymoon souvenirs,
tickets, brochures and other
printed ephemera.

LEFT Label your storage boxes
neatly for easy reference.

keepsakes

Those once vital check-lists, guest lists, swatches, tear sheets, magazine articles and other paraphernalia that you accumulated when planning your wedding will all acquire their own special meaning in time. Preserve your memories by sorting them into carefully labelled scrapbooks, boxes and files, for even the tiniest scrap of wrapping paper or scrawled love note will one day be an irreplaceable and sentimental keepsake. You can also allocate separate storage boxes for your wedding cards, letters and the photographs that didn't quite make it into the albums.

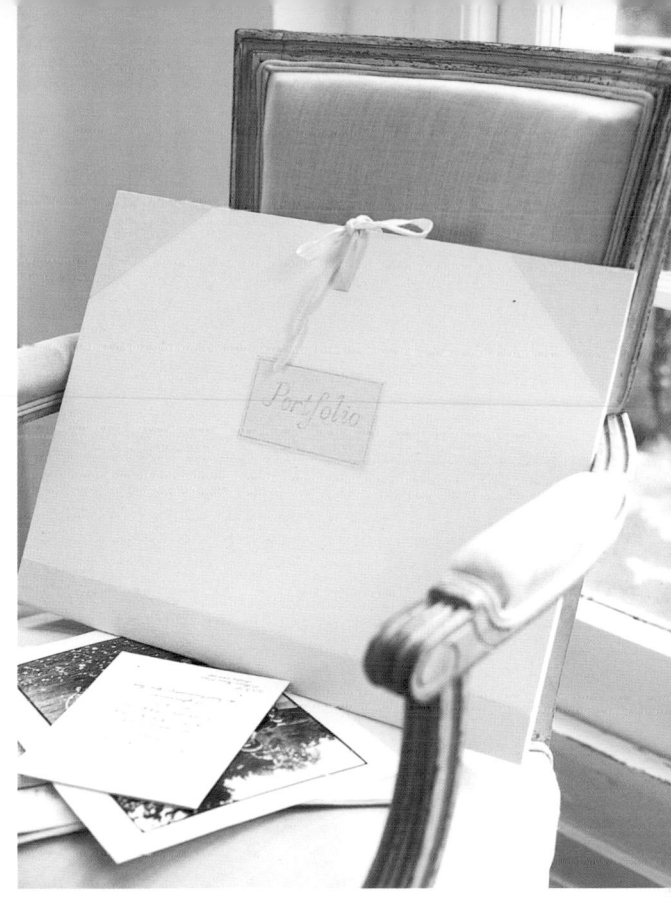

ABOVE A simple tie-up portfolio, either bought or made from a folded sheet of mounting board and trimmed with contrasting corners and spine, is the best way to store large presentation photographs, mood boards or sketches for your wedding dress. Make a label bearing the date of your wedding or your monograms.

LEFT Turn your favourite bits and pieces into a nostalgic artwork. Glue rows of luggage labels to a plain stretched canvas (available from good art shops), then display tiny photos, a sachet of rice, beads, buckles, dried flowers and ribbon samples by tying them on to the strings.

PROJECT 12
scrapbook

After a wedding, there is always a huge stack of ephemera. In addition to all the cards and photographs, there are endless bits and pieces, all of which have their own particular significance – from receipts and brochures to pressed flowers, fabric swatches and gift tags. Keep them all safe and sound in this pretty fabric-covered scrapbook, and group items together to make pages of particular memories. Label and caption everything so that you can look back and remember all those significant details in years to come.

MATERIALS & EQUIPMENT
Spiral-bound scrapbook • Ruler or tape measure
Linen fabric for the cover • Fabric for the lining
Scissors • Double-sided adhesive tape
50cm length of medium-width ribbon • Stick-on dots
Scraps of toning cotton fabric and felt
Selection of buttons, sequins and ribbon
Matching embroidery threads • PVA adhesive
White fabric

1   For the cover you will need a rectangle of fabric 4cm deeper than your scrapbook and 6cm wider than the open book. Fix a length of double-sided tape to the wrong side of each edge and fold over, short edges first.

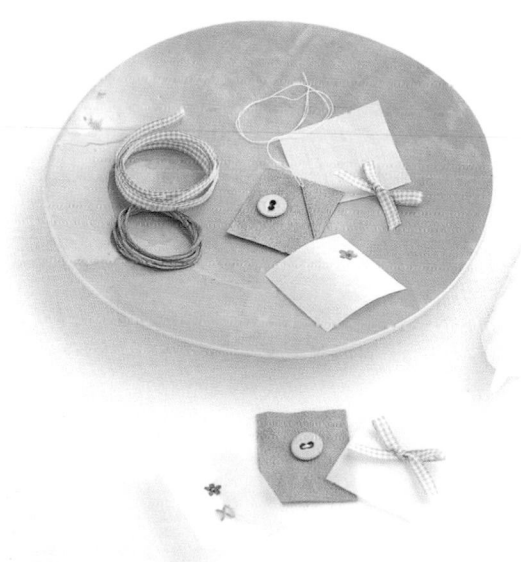

2 Cut the ribbon in two halves and trim the ends. Stick a piece to the centre front and back using adhesive dots. Cut two rectangles of lining fabric 2cm shorter and 1cm wider than the inside cover and fix in place with double-sided tape.

3 Cut six patches from the scraps of fabric, in various sizes from 3 x 4cm rectangles to 4cm squares. Sew a button to one and flower sequins to another. Tie a length of narrow ribbon into a small bow and sew this to the third patch.

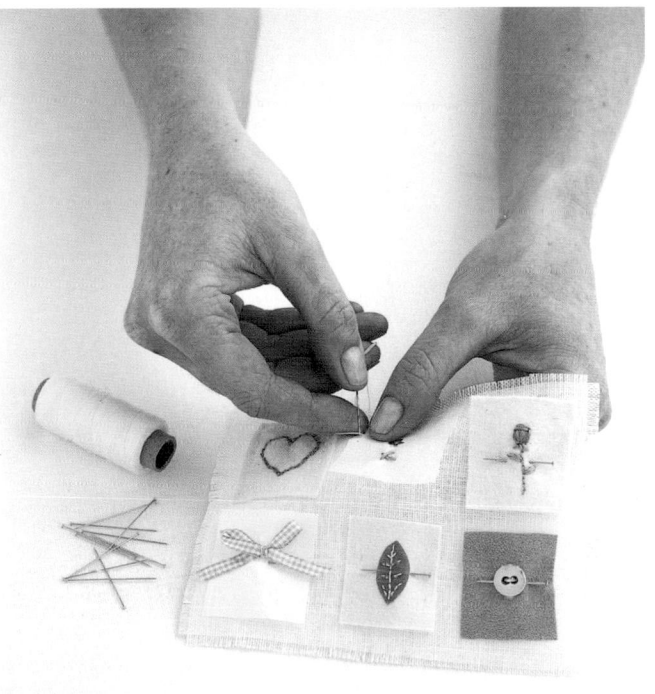

4 Cut a felt leaf and sew on to the fourth patch with contrasting embroidery thread, to form a pattern of veins. Stitch a small pink heart outline and a tiny rosebud with a green stem on the remaining patches.

5 Cut a rectangle of white fabric, approximately 12 x 24cm. Fray the edges, then pin the patches in place. Stitch them down with matching sewing thread. Fix the panel on to the front of the scrapbook with a thin layer of PVA adhesive.

sources

BEADS

THE BEAD SHOP
21 Tower Street
London WC2H 9NS
020 7240 0931
www.beadshop.co.uk
An unsurpassed selection of
beads, wire and findings.

BEADYKATE
01942 496238
www.beadykate.com
An unusual range of natural
beads: freshwater pearls, coral
and tumbled gemstones.

CREATIVE BEADCRAFT
(Ells and Farrier)
20 Beak Street
London W1F 9RE
01494 715606
www.creativebeadcraft.co.uk
Beads, sequins, pearls,
diamantés and more.

DELICATE STITCHES
339 Kentish Town Road
London NW5 2TJ
0870 203 2323
www.londonbeadco.co.uk
Embroidery threads, ribbons
and coloured wires, along with
hundreds of decorative beads
and sequins.

BUTTONS

THE BUTTON QUEEN
19 Marylebone Lane
London W1V 2NF
020 7935 1505
www.thebuttonqueen.co.uk
A charming shop with a unique
selection of antique and
modern buttons.

RIBBONMOON
www.ribbonmoon.co.uk
Online haberdashery shop,
with over 3500 different
buttons to choose from.

CAKES

GATEAUX DE MARIAGE
020 8674 6086
www.gateauxdemariage.co.uk
Croquembouche, gateaux and
traditional wedding cakes from
French pastry chef Jean-Marc
Fouque.

KONDITOR AND COOK
22 Cornwall Road
London SE1 8TW
Call 020 7261 0456 or visit
www.konditorandcook.co.uk for
details of their other branches.
Unconventional wedding cakes
plus delicious patisserie.

**LITTLE VENICE CAKE
COMPANY**
15 Manchester Mews
London W1U 2DX
020 7486 5252
www.lvcc.co.uk
Bespoke wedding cakes.

**THE LITTLE WEDDING CAKE
COMPANY**
www.littlecakes.co.uk
A range of personalized
miniature wedding cakes.

SAVOIR DESIGN
The Garden House
2 Vardens Road
London SW11 1RH
020 8877 9770
www.savoirdesign.co.uk
Exquisite wedding cakes
specially created by celebrity
pastry chef Eric Lanlard.

CANDLES AND LIGHTING

E. & S. CHURCHILL
15G Queensway
Enfield
Middlesex EN3 4SL
020 8804 1444
eschurchill.co.uk
Hand-made beeswax candles
in a wide range of colours.

LOVES ME LOVES ME KNOT
www.lovesmelovesmeknot.co.uk
Storm lanterns, round garden
lanterns and hanging tealight
holders for outdoor
celebrations. Also strings of
flower fairy lights, mini
sparklers, candle sand and
floating flower candles.

PRICE'S CANDLES
100 York Road
London SW11 3RU
020 7924 6336
www.prices-candles.co.uk
Wide range of beeswax, pillar
and dinner candles.

R.K. ALLISTON
173 New Kings Road
London SW6 4SW
020 7751 0077
www.rkalliston.com
Citronella candles in terracotta
pots, glass and paper lanterns.

CONFETTI

FOREVER MEMORIES
01384 878111
www.forevermemories.co.uk
Metallic and paper confetti, as
well as freeze-dried and fabric
rose petals. Also favour boxes
and personalized ribbon.

PASSION FOR PETALS
01404 811467
www.passionforpetals.com
Bougainvillaea petal confetti in
every shade of pink, as well as
freeze-dried rose petals. Also
flower seeds for use as
favours and round glass-
topped metallic favour cases.

THE REAL FLOWER PETAL
CONFETTI COMPANY
01386 555045
www.confettidirect.co.uk
Hand-picked delphinium petal
confetti in several colours,
dried naturally on the farm.

TRULY MADLY DEEPLY
0870 120 0316
www.truly.madly.deeply.biz
Real flower-petal confetti,
beaded candle surrounds and
personalized chocolate favours.

CRAFT SUPPLIES

CLARK CRAFT PRODUCTS
ONLINE
08000 371420
www.clarkcrafts.co.uk
Paper, card, hole punches, rub-
on letters and numbers, glitter,
glue and general haberdashery.

COWLING AND WILCOX
26–28 Broadwick Street
London W1V 1FG
020 7734 9556
www.cowlingandwilcox.com
Art materials, including
polymer and air-drying clay.

HOBBYCRAFT
Call 0800 027 2387 or visit
www.hobbycraft.co.uk for
details of your nearest store.
Craft superstores selling,
among 60,000 other lines, air-
drying clay and favour boxes.

FABRICS AND
HABERDASHERY

BRIDAL LACE
5 Belmont Close
Hucknall
Nottingham NG15 6DJ
0116 963 1360
www.bridallace.com
Chiffons, silks, organzas,
duchesse satins and fine lace.

BROADWICK SILKS
9–11 Broadwick Street
London W1F 0DB
020 7734 3320
Fabulous bridal fabrics
including net and beaded silks.

HARRINGTON BRIDAL
FABRICS AND LACES
Harrington Mills
Leopold Street
Long Eaton
Nottingham NG10 4QE
0115 946 0766
Mail-order satins, brocades,
chiffon, veiling and lace fabrics.
Ring for samples and price list.

JOHN LEWIS
Call 08456 049 049 or visit
www.johnlewis.com for details
of your nearest store.
Their haberdashery
departments carry lace, felt,
pearl-headed pins, buttons,
ribbons, feathers and silk
flowers along with a good
selection of dressmaking and
furnishing fabrics including
linens and silks.

KATE FORMAN FABRICS
www.kateforman.co.uk
Vintage-style floral furnishing
fabrics.

MACCULLOCH AND WALLIS
25–26 Dering Street
London W1R 0BH
020 7629 0311
Suppliers of haberdashery and
millinery accessories for over a
hundred years.

NEW RAINBOW TEXTILES
98 The Broadway
Southall
Middlesex UB1 1QF
020 8574 1494
Fabulous array of fabulous
Indian braids, silks and sari
fabrics.

SILK SHADES
The Lace Market Centre
3–5 High Pavement
Nottingham NG1 1HF
0115 988 1848
www.silk-shades.co.uk
A wide selection of silk fabrics.

FAVOURS

CARTE BLANCHE
CREATIONS
01535 664494
www.carteblanchecreations.co.uk
Gorgeous favour packaging,
including zinc buckets, tins,
Cellophane bags and hand-
made boxes, plus lots of
goodies to go inside them.

THE CHOCOLATE TRADING
COMPANY
www.chocolatetradingco.com
Foil-wrapped chocolate hearts
and colourful sugar-coated
heart-shaped chocolate
dragees. Also chocolate coins
that can be personalized.

MAISON BLANC
62 Hampstead High Street
London NW3 1QH
020 7731 8338
www.maisonblanc.co.uk
Visit the website or call
020 8838 0848 for details of
their other branches.
French pâtisserie, chocolates
and little treats, including
colourful lollipops, marzipan,
nougat and sugared almonds
that make perfect favours.

ROCOCO CHOCOLATES
321 King's Road
London SW3 5EP
020 7352 5857
www.rococochocolates.com
Beautifully packaged Swiss
chocolates, truffles, nougat and
other novelties. Mail order
available.

SIMPLY BEAUTIFUL
FAVOURS
01285 862717
www.sbfavours.co.uk
Stylish boxes, bags, fillers
(including sugared and silvered
almonds), along with
accessories from which you
can create your own favours.

THE VERY NICE COMPANY
www.theverynicecompany.com
Perspex containers, favour
boxes in all shapes and sizes,
lottery-ticket envelopes, bags,
bottles of bubbles and
biodegradable confetti.

WITH LOVE FROM
www.withlovefrom.co.uk
Favour boxes, wedding cake-
shaped candles, craft boxes
and fabric and paper gift bags.

FLORISTRY SUPPLIES

W. & M. SMITH
Moat Farm
Middlewood Green
Stowmarket IP14 5HG
www.wandmsmith.co.uk
Comprehensive range of
floristry equipment, including
wire, tape, corsage pins,
candles, silk flowers and oasis
wreath frames.

SOLSTUF
0121 243 6067
www.solstuf.co.uk
Loose fragrant lavender and
rose petals sold in bulk. Also
rosebuds, bunches of lavender
and delphinium-petal confetti.

PAPERS AND STATIONERY

BLACK MOUSE
www.blackmouse.co.uk
DIY wedding stationery – a
range of materials including
card blanks, pre-cut inserts,
decorative items and mix and
match envelopes. Full
instructions are provided.

FAULKINER FINE PAPERS
76 Southampton Row
London WC1B 4AR
020 7831 1151
Suppliers of traditional hand-
made and marbled papers.

LIBERTY CRAFTS
020 8686 0313
www.libertycrafts.co.uk
Card-making materials, with
good range of mulberry and
other textured papers.

PAPERCHASE
Call 020 7467 6200 or visit
www.paperchase.co.uk for
details of your nearest store.
Seventy outlets nationwide
selling the definitive range of
stationery, art materials, gift-
wrap and paper of all
descriptions.

THE PAPERSHED
www.papershed.com
Large selection of specialist
paper products, including
products specially designed for
weddings.

SCRIBBLER
15 Shorts Gardens
London WC2 9AT
020 7836 9688
www.scribbler.co.uk
Cards, gift wrap, fun gifts and
quirky gadgets.

RIBBONS AND TRIMS

WENDY CUSHIING
TRIMMINGS
G7 Chelsea Harbour Design
Centre
Chelsea Harbour
London SW10 0XE
020 7351 5796
www.wendycushing.com
Exquisite furnishing trimmings,
including braids, bead fringes
and tassels.

ODDITIES ANTIQUES
www.odditiesantiques.com
Vintage ribbons, buttons,
beads, fabrics and braids

VV ROULEAUX
6 Marylebone High Street
London W1U 4NJ
020 7224 5179
Highly desirable selection of
ribbons (including Mokuba),
velvet and silk flowers, beaded
wires and other decorative
accessories.

SPINA DESIGN
020 7328 5274
www.spinadesign.co.uk
Luxurious hand-made
trimmings, tassels and tie-
backs.

TEMPTATION ALLEY
359–361 Portobello Road
London W10 5SA
020 8964 2004
An Aladdin's cave of every kind
of trim, from diamanté to
sequins and feathers.

WEDDING SPECIALISTS

CONFETTI
80–81 Tottenham Court Road
London W1T 4TE
020 7436 7177
www.confetti.co.uk
A wonderful specialist store,
with a mail-order service. A
good starting point with lots of
ideas for making stationery,
favours and table decorations.

templates

To make a template, either use a photocopier to copy the desired template onto heavy paper, or trace the pattern and transfer it to heavy paper or card. Cut out the template, pin it to the wrong side of your fabric, then cut out. You can trace round the template in faint pencil if preferred.

picture credits

Key: ph= photographer, a=above, b=below, r=right, l=left, c=centre.

All projects photographed by Carolyn Barber. All other photographs by Polly Wreford unless otherwise stated.

Page 1 etched crystal goblets from Evertrading, spiral plates from Designers Guild, damask tablecloth from Antique Linen Company, pink and blue damask napkins from Thomas Goode; 2 condiments, cutlery and place-card holders from Thomas Goode, Stuart Crystal wineglasses from Waterford Crystal, china from Richard Ginori; 3 & 4 ph Carolyn Barber; 5 rustic wire basket from Fenwick, hand-made paper from Paperchase, white fabric petals from Confetti, wire-edge ribbon from VV Rouleaux; 6 cake box from Bomboniere, fabric flower from VV Rouleaux; 8 three-tiered cake decorated with icing pearls designed by Eric at Savoir Design, pink satin ribbon from VV Rouleaux; 10 all & 11bl ph Craig Fordham; 11ar 28 Portland Place, London; 12al 28 Portland Place, London; 12br braided fabric and pearl-headed dressmaker's pins from John Lewis; 12–13a, 13ar, 13br, 14, 15 all ph Craig Fordham; 18–19 all ph Craig Fordham except 18ac; 20ac, 20–21a, 20–21b, 21ac & 21ar all ph Craig Fordham; 24al 28 Portland Place, London, cutlery and pot from Christofle UK Ltd, crystal wineglass from Evertrading; 24–25 etched goblets from Oka, cutlery from IKEA; 26l Skywood House, Middlesex, designed by architect Graham Phillips, cups and saucers from Wedgwood, similar cylindrical flower vase available from IKEA and Habitat, blue-rimmed china from Royal Worcester, four-tiered cake from Savoir Design; 26ar shot glasses from Habitat; 28al crystal wine glass from Evertrading; 28ar etched crystal goblets from Evertrading, spiral plates from Designers Guild, damask tablecloth from Antique Linen Company, pink and blue damask napkins from Thomas Goode; 29 floral china table setting from Richard Ginori, engraved goblet set from Evertrading, silver shallow vase from Kenneth Turner, chairs from Nordic Style; 30br chairs and cushions from Nordic Style; 31br 28 Portland Place, London; 34 cake from Savoir Design, pearl-beaded braid from VV Rouleaux; 36l cakes from Savoir Design; 36r cake from Savoir Design, pearl-beaded braid and organza chiffon flower from VV Rouleaux, crystal champagne flutes from William Yeoward Crystal, china from Royal Worcester; 37 Skywood House, Middlesex designed by architect Graham Phillips/4-tiered cake decorated with icing pearls designed by Eric at Savoir Design; 39l cake from Savoir Design; 39r cake designed by Makiko Sakita at Confetti; 40a cake from Savoir Design, butterflies from C. Best at Nine Elms Market, Vauxhall, gold-striped ribbon and sequinned butterflies from VV Rouleaux, gold-rimmed glassware from Thomas Goode; 40b embroidered linen coasters from the Irish Linen Company; 41 cakes from Savoir Design; 43 cakes from Waitrose, pastry fork from Antique Designs Ltd; 44 napkin holder decoration from VV Rouleaux; 45a napkins and gilt hoop napkin holders from Thomas Goode; 45bc silver fretwork ring napkin holders from Grange, pewter bowl from Kenneth Turner; 45br silver-rimmed china from Royal Worcester; 46a embroidered napkins from Antique Designs Ltd; 46b white porcelain rose napkin holder from Thomas Goode; 47al damask napkin and beaded tassel napkin holder from Thomas Goode, patterned plates from Christofle; 47ar silk tassels with mink pompoms (made to hold keys) used as napkin holders from Robbie Spina; 47c scalloped plates from Designers Guild, flower braid napkin holder from Jane Churchill; 48, 49a, 49bl & 49bc all ph David Loftus; 49br patterned china from Richard Ginori, blue etched glass plate from IKEA; 52al champagne flutes from Evertrading; 52ar hand-made paper from Paperchase; 52b spotty cups and saucers from Richard Ginori; 54ar porcelain bunny place-card holder from Herend Porcelain; 58b crystal cake stand from Baccarat, green glass baubles from Paperchase; 59br patterned china and silver coffee pot from Christofle; 62 flower and beaded garland candleholder from VV Rouleaux; 63 cream painted wire baskets from Fenwick; 67ar glass holders from Habitat, mirror from C. Best at Nine Elms Market, Vauxhall; 67br tray edged with glass beads and frosted glass votives from Fenwick; 68ar glass lanterns from R.K. Alliston; 69al fretwork lantern from Fenwick; 69ac white wire lantern from Fenwick; 69ar glass candleholders from Menu A/S; 69b Chinese lanterns from IKEA; 72 similar favour boxes from Confetti and Bomboniere, plate from Habitat; 74ar & br truffles and gold-wrapped chocolate hearts all from Rococo chocolates; 75 hand-made biscuits from Savoir Designs; 78a similar favour boxes from Confetti and Bomboniere; 79al corrugated favour boxes from Bomboniere, ribbons from VV Rouleaux; 80al candy-pink favour box from Paperchase, ribbon from VV Rouleaux, floral gold-rimmed plates from Royal Worcester; 80ac coloured etched wineglass from William Yeoward Crystal, ribbon from VV Rouleaux; 80cr wire garland of tiny glass hearts from VV Rouleaux; 80b all plates and translucent onyx bowl from Thomas Goode; 80–81a white bone china from Royal Copenhagen, embroidered handkerchief from the Irish Linen Company; 81ac Sandringham plate from Royal Worcester, floral handkerchief from the Irish Linen Company; 81ar silver tin plant pot from the Netherlands Flower Bulb Information Centre; 81b ribbon and silk flower from VV Rouleaux, gold box from Paperchase, gold-rimmed china from Royal Worcester; 84 rustic wire basket from Fenwick, hand-made paper from Paperchase, white fabric petals from Confetti, wire-edge ribbon from VV Rouleaux; 86ac flower-petal confetti from Confetti; 86-87a flower-petal confetti from Confetti, white-painted wire basket from Fenwick; 88b embroidered linen sachets and embroidered table linen from the Irish Linen Company; 90al embroidered silk bags from Grange.